COPING

W I T H

Being Physically Challenged

Linda Lee Ratto

D1522002

THE ROSEN PUBLISHING GROUP, INC./NEW YORK

Published in 1991 by The Rosen Publishing Group, Inc.
29 East 21st Street, New York, NY 10010

First Edition

Library of Congress Cataloging-in-Publication Data
Ratto, Linda Lee.
    Coping with being physically challenged / Linda Lee Ratto.
        p.   cm.
    Includes bibliographical references and index.
    Summary: Gives guidance for young people on handling physical disabilities, with emphasis on problems faced by teens in school and dating.
    ISBN 0–8239–1344–9 :
    1. Physically handicapped teenagers—United States—Life skills guides—Juvenile literature.   [1. Physically handicapped.   2. Life skills.]   I. Title.
HV888.5.R37   1991   90–23699
649'.151—dc20   CIP
                                                                 AC

Manufactured in the United States of America

In heartfelt gratitude, this book is dedicated to my David, Courtney, Eric, and Ryan, my shining stars.

ABOUT THE AUTHOR ◇

Linda Lee Ratto was raised in Ellenville, a very small town in the Catskill Mountains of New York. She is an educator with a Bachelor of Science degree in English and Education and a Master's in Reading Education from the University of New York.

The title of her Master's thesis was "Left and Right Handedness: Can the Absence of a Limb Affect the Learning of a Child?" She was afraid that a child born without a limb would lack sensory stimulation on that side of the body and thus be deficient in some way. Happily, her personal theory was proved wrong by her research. Medical and educational studies suggested that her first baby, a daughter born with one hand, would have a high chance of being intellectually superior. Her findings show a need for the brain to operate in two modes in order to do the simplest task: operating with one hand, and with a prosthesis. This necessity fosters challenges and extra stimulation for the brain. An update on this information: her daughter just received the Principal's Award: the highest award given, for academic as well as civic achievement, for her entire fifth grade. The word is challenge, not handicap!

Mrs. Ratto has been a counselor for over seven years. She is a national public speaker on many issues such as parenting handicapped children, educating oneself to be a partner with medical personnel, coping with cancer, and coping with trauma.

She has spoken for such organizations as: the American Academy of Orthotists and Prosthetists, Parents of Amputee Children Together (PACT), both American Societies of Plastic and Reconstructive Surgeons and Nurses, and the American Cancer Society. She organizes seminars, teaches adult courses, and has been advocating education of the patient on several television and radio programs. She has just finished publishing medical research on the psychological aspects of cancer.

Having taught all levels of elementary school, Mrs. Ratto is presently teaching 8th Grade Reading at her daughter's school. She lives in Georgia with her husband and three children, Courtney, Eric, and Ryan. Recently, Ryan was blinded in one eye in an accident. She is writing about that experience as well.

Contents

	Preface	viii
1	Being Physically Challenged	1
2	Six Steps of a Healthy Grief Process	9
3	Not Sympathy, But Understanding	15
4	Self-Worth: The Importance of a Positive Self-Image	25
5	Personal Independence and Friends, Too	30
6	Peers, Adolescent Changes, and Dating	34
7	Adaptation: Everyday Frustrations	39
8	Sorrow	46
9	A Partnership with Medical Personnel	53
10	Fear and Anger: The AIDS Crisis	63
11	How to Keep a Diary	68
12	Siblings' Feelings	72
13	Academic Talent	76
14	We, the Leaders	82
15	Life Is a Challenge — for Everyone	85
16	Ways to Face Each Day — with Happiness	87
	Glossary	89
	Resource List	93
	Index	100

PREFACE

There are always reasons why we do the things we do. When my first child was born without a left hand, I cried. Then I began to write. She's almost twelve now, so I've been writing a long time. I write about our experiences and feelings. I write about the young people we meet in our clinic and hospital visits. I am a real mother, and my daughter is a real person. She is called handicapped by professionals and "regular citizens" alike. I have never felt that she couldn't at least try. This book is written in the hope of convincing others, at the very least, to try.

CHAPTER 1

Being Physically Challenged

COURTNEY

I was born with only one hand. We haven't been able to find out why, so we (my family and I) decided to just accept it as my challenge and go from there. I am a congenital amputee, meaning I was *born* handicapped. I have to say, though, that I don't *feel* handicapped. I would rather say I am physically challenged. I never think I can't do something, I just go for it. I give *anything* a try. Yes, some of the things I try are made unusually difficult because of the lack of two hands and ten fingers. I get extremely frustrated. Sometimes everyday life is just plain hard. But when I finally do something well, like the high-balance beam in gymnastics, my heart flies with happiness. Maybe my physical challenge makes me especially proud of myself when I do something well. Some things sure take a long, long time to learn. But my accomplishments are pretty sweet from my point of view.

RYAN

I went blind in one eye last year. I've had six eye operations. I'm all healed, but my retina (the seeing part of the eye) isn't working. I can't see anything but light and dark with that eye. When I first wake up in the morning, I forget. I rub my eyes, still half asleep, thinking that I'll just clear my left eye and the cloud of gray will melt away. It doesn't. I bump into things I never did before. I can't tell what's coming on that left side. I either have to turn really fast or get hit by baseballs that come from that direction. I wear safety glasses to protect my sighted eye and to keep objects from getting into both my eyes. I think I'm getting used to life with one eye, but I still hate that this happened to me. I'm called handicapped. If I wanted to be an astronaut or a pilot, they wouldn't let me now. That's handicapped, and I hate it.

THE WORDS HANDICAPPED AND CHALLENGED

The dictionary definition of *handicap* is as follows:

a disadvantage that makes achievement unusually difficult; especially a physical disability.

The prefix *dis-* before a word means: do the opposite of; deprive of.

On the other hand, the definition of *challenge* is:

a stimulating or interesting task or problem.

That certainly is a more optimistic way of looking at the physical disabilities some of us have.

There are two main types of physically challenged people: those born the way they are, and those who have contracted a disease or have had an accident. This book, while pointing out the uniquely different points of view of these people, will explain their similarities. Whatever our own personal deficiencies, we all want to be treated fairly and with care. This book will explain how you can be treated well by treating yourself with kindness first. There are many steps, many paths toward a satisfying life. Read on and see if one or more of those paths fits you.

TRAUMA

To further explain basically normal people who have become disabled, the word *trauma* must be introduced. These persons have gone through an acute, life-altering trauma.

Trauma is defined in the dictionary as:

> *a disordered mental or behavioral state resulting from mental or emotional stress or physical injury.*

Pay attention to the word *disordered*. The order of the person's life has become changed, out-of-normal. Trauma is not a large word, but it represents incredible change. That change can be permanent. It affects every single thing the person does, especially at first. Most of the time, the change is not of the person's own choice. (There are people who use drugs or hurt themselves by choice. They can end up disabled and have yet another group of troubles just as traumatic as those of the accident or disease victim. They have to deal with the guilt of their own poor choices.)

It is a challenge to truly understand the inside of a physically challenged person's life. We all have shortcomings, things we would love to change about ourselves. Whatever your personal handicap, read the sketches of the real young people below and try to put yourself in their emotional and physical shoes.

JESSICA

Jessica broke her arm roller skating. A hard cast was prescribed for six very long weeks. She felt incredibly handicapped. She could no longer feed herself without looking like a baby who had forgotten her bib. You see, she broke her dominant writing arm. The day the cast was removed was the beginning of a new life for her. She woke every morning looking at her healed arm with great appreciation. She had more energy to do things, simply because she could do them with two arms! Jessica matured. She learned to see life from more than one point of view.

DARRYL

Darryl needed surgery. He had been sick almost all his life: sore throats, swollen glands, and millions of gallons of antibiotics and nasal decongestants (He could never swallow tablets — his throat was always so raw.) were part of his everyday life. The doctors said he needed a tonsillectomy. He was in the hospital for three days, home for two weeks. In the hospital it was frightening. Other people were in control of his body. He felt like an invalid. But gradually he was able to swallow ice cream without pain. He went home. Slowly, he walked around his house, feeling better. The weekend before he was to go back to school, he was at his desk catching up on homework. He noticed that he wasn't the least bit tired. He swallowed. He did not feel one spot of soreness. So this is what life is like! I love feeling good! And his entire attitude toward what he could do and wanted to do changed! He took advantage of his newfound health and made the *high* Honor Roll in eighth grade. He grew for the better. He learned from his handicap.

That is the challenged feeling, and that is the way to live your days: learning through a crisis and coming out of it with a better outlook on your life. Learning and understanding lead to the acceptance of other people's differences, too. That can only help society to grow happier.

FEEL GOOD ABOUT YOURSELF

In the nineties we should rejoice at the stand the United States government is taking on the rights of disabled Americans. The summer of 1990 brought us an addition to the laws of the land, making it illegal to discriminate against a person because of his or her disability. Hiring of people must be based on *ABILITY*. Accentuate the positive. You *are* able.

To deal with a handicap, one must first feel that the person inside is worth a lot. Let's go back to when you were a fresh new baby. No one can disagree: Every single baby is good. Babies are new. Although they cry and make messes, they are not bad. You were a baby. The inside of you has just grown up a little. You may not be perfect. But inside, that big baby is still a good person. Remember that, and show it to others. *Like* yourself. You are a fresh, unique, new person! Not one person is like you. That is exciting!

FIND A PERSON TO BE ON YOUR SIDE

You don't have to do it alone. Parents and family can help you keep a positive, go-for-it attitude. Loved ones are extremely important in dealing with any problem or challenge. If you do not have a special group of supporters in your life, it's time to go out and get a couple of people on your side. Take a moment to look at the people around you. Perhaps you are not letting them love and support you. Perhaps you need to appreciate those close relatives and accepting friends. Here are some steps to help you find people who can help you feel more positive about *you*.

1. Talk to a family member you haven't talked to lately.
2. Have a talk with a favorite teacher.
3. When you go to the doctor or clinic, try to talk to one new person, perhaps someone your own age or someone who has problems similar to yours. Talk to your doctor or therapist.
4. Write to an organization, a newsletter, or even a local support group asking for printed material on your special differences. (See Resources at the end of this book.) Ask about special meetings, family days, and other fun being organized for you.
5. Read. Read information you've received in the mail. Read books on any type of handicap. People with differences have many similar feelings.
6. Write down your thoughts in a diary. Perhaps choose a friend to share diaries with. Or simply keep the journal private: only for your eyes and your heart.

Glance at the chart below. Have you ever felt any of those emotions?

HANDICAPPING FEELINGS	NEWLY LEARNED FEELINGS
Helplessness	I'm a good person; I can live through this
Out-of-control	I'll try a few things
Sad	I can do some things
Depressed	It's okay to be sad, for a while . . .
Mad	
Angry	I feel happy when I get some little thing done
Furious	It's okay to be mad, but not to take it out on my family and others

Why not someone else?	Why not me? I'll be fine. I can learn
	    from this. I know people who care
	    who can help me.

TIPS ON HOW TO FEEL GOOD ABOUT YOURSELF TODAY!

If you try one of these a day, you should start to feel better than you did last week. If your mind is happy, your body is happier as well.

1. Get up with a brand-new-start attitude.
   Yesterday is gone. Mistakes and sadness should not be carried over to another day.
2. Forgive yourself and others.
   No one is perfect. Love yourself and others.
3. Look in the mirror at a favorite part of your face and smile.
   Do not focus on the pimple; focus on your beautiful eyes, hair, teeth, lips, eyelashes!
4. Tell yourself: I am beautiful, I am a worthwhile person.
   Every person is special; every person has unique goodness.

5. Breathe in, and try!
   Do not set limits today: Try something new, or try an old, difficult challenge again, with your new attitude.

It is a new day: a new morning, a new afternoon, and a brand-new night. There is time to take opportunities, time to succeed.

And don't forget to pat yourself on the back!

CHAPTER 2

Six Steps of a Healthy Grief Process

PHYSICIANS OF THE MIND AND BODY AGREE

According to thousands of physicians, surgeons, psychologists, and psychiatrists, we all need to go through some basic human stages when we are faced with a shocking loss. In this chapter we mean the loss of a person's normal health. But the stages are the same for any of us if we face the death of a close friend or relative. When we are faced with the death of the person we *used* to be (or, in the case of congenital handicaps, *could* have been) eventually we have to begin anew. We have to go on. Yet we also have to give ourselves time to be sad. Doctors believe that a person who does not grow through all six stages will not grow properly. He or she will remain stuck. That is serious and must be looked into. We must all grow and change in our lives, or our minds and emotions will become unhealthy. That is bad not only for the handicapped person but also for his or her entire family and group of friends.

Following are the six basic stages of growth through a traumatic experience:

1. *Shock*
   Not me!
   Why me?
   Leave me alone!
2. *Anger*
   At God!
   At relatives and friends.
   At doctors.
   At anyone in sight.
3. *Let me make a deal*
   If I am good, God will heal me.
   If I am a better and nicer person, I'll get back to normal.
   I did that wrong, so this is my punishment.
   I'll never do it again; just let me be myself again.
4. *Sadness*
   Overwhelming reality.
   Never-before-experienced levels of sorrow.
   Grief at the personal loss (death of the past self).
5. *Accepting reality*
   This is it, the way it is going to be.
   I'm not angry or depressed.
6. *Hope*
   What can I do to get better than this? (We can always improve.)
   I think I can live!
   I bet I can live well!
   I'm even going to be *HAPPY* sometimes!

If a handicapped person can grow through all these stages, his or her mind will be ready to cope with daily life.

MAX

Although I was born with no legs because my mother took the drug Thalidomide, I am always growing and changing. True, I don't know what it's like to have legs, but I can figure out how great it would be. Being in high school has put me right out on the firing line. Some days it's a war just to get through gym class. War with my body, that is. Walking on leg prostheses is tough. I'm over 180 pounds of active muscle. I lift weights, play basketball. But if I get a simple little rash on the ends of my legs, I can't wear my prostheses. That means I can't work out because I need crutches or my wheelchair to get around.

Even though I was born this way, I find myself going in and out of the stages of grief many times in my life. It's those little moments of grief: They become traumas for me. Any new situation is a time of anger, frustration, and sadness. I do wish I had two legs. It does bother me. It is a source of personal agony for me. A new school, a new class, a new club or church group are all situations that push me into explaining about myself all over again. Moving is another main time of change. It is upsetting, filled with people who know nothing about me. I have to educate them, make them feel comfortable, because I am rare: a minority that many people have never met. I get tired. I am weary of the teasing if I don't take time to fill in my new classmates or neighbors. That can trigger anger in me, old anger with new faces. I can be crabby, taking my thoughts of "Why me?" out on my parents and brothers. I spend time in my room blaming the new kids I don't know yet because I'm tired. I wish they just knew about me magically. It's ridiculous when I look back on those times, because right now I feel great. But when I am in the middle of overwhelming sadness over my leglessness, it does not seem one bit silly.

CHANGE

We change every day. We think we can't change. We think we don't *want* to change. We think we know exactly how it will be if we do change. And yet change sneaks up on us all the time, day in and day out. Take hair, for instance: You get a great cut. Every day your hair grows. Slowly you change the way you style it because of the new growth. You may not notice it for about a month. Then one day you notice that your hair is too long. How did *that* happen? Daily change and growth; we simply adjust.

MELANIE

I personally think the people who were born normal have it a lot harder when a handicapping event happens in their lives. They have to be shocked into changing their lives. That is not easy. I haven't had that kind of shock. I was born blind. I am used to it.

JASON

Life is tougher than normal for me. I lost my legs fighting for America. I'm twenty-two. I can't be in the Army any more. I had planned on being a career officer. I was in combat in South America. Now all I have is medical discharge papers. Daily reminders, everyday little things send a handicapped person into depression. Sympathy is not what I need. I'm pushing for understanding. Put yourself in my shoes. Then, whatever your life is like, you can always be grateful it isn't like mine. I know I'm thankful for what I *can* do. I'm glad I'm alive.

KELLY

I'm a congenital left-leg amputee. I think arm amputees have it a whole lot harder than I do. I can fool people. I can hide my leg prosthesis. The arm amputees have to have their prosthesis right out in the open. Even if they wear long sleeves, you can see their hook. I'm glad I have two hands and just one foot.

SHAWN

When I think I am the most depressed double-arm amputee in the world, I go for an extra two-mile jog. I'm a junior champion marathon runner. In spite of having absolutely nothing but shoulders to attach my two hook prostheses to, I get through my angry, depressed times by doing what I love to do best: *jog*. I'd rather be a bilateral-arm amputee, because I'd rather be able to run. No prostheses to weigh these legs down!

TOBY

People used to ask my mother, "How do you stand it, going to all those hospitals with names like: For Crippled Children?" I heard her say, "Actually, after getting to know those kids and their never-say-die spirit, *my* life is a dream!" That's basically the way I think. Yes, I have MS. I live in a wheelchair most of the time because my legs went numb when I was only eighteen years old. I'm twenty-three now. I finished a two-year college program while living at home. My plan is to live on the campus of the university an hour from here. I'm going to be a doctor and find a cure for multiple sclerosis. I have some great days when I almost forget that my legs don't work. Some of the patients at the clinic have gone blind. I get very scared. I could get worse. My disease appears to be in remission. Only my legs have been affected so far. My mind has no boundaries!

Everyone's point of view is affected by the things he or she has to live through. Going in and out of the stages of grief is normal, healthy growth for the mind and the body.

CHAPTER ◇ 3

Not Sympathy,
But Understanding

When a person goes to the hospital, an outpouring of attention floods onto him or her. Balloons, flowers, cookies, and candy seem to come out of the walls. The new patient, although feeling ill, is happy for the attention. Any human being thrives on extra love. Being the center of positive feelings is wonderful.

The physically challenged person has problems with extra attention. In fact, most of them crave to be allowed to melt into the classroom pot, to be unnoticed. To be part of the norm is their dream.

JUSTIN

There are times when I would love to tear my hearing aids right out of my skull and throw them at the next person who even *looks* my way. I don't want anyone's attention. I want to be looked at for me, a decent-looking junior in high school with a driver's license and a fairly new used car. I want to date a girl and not

have to explain my life and losing most of my hearing.
I just want to be left alone. I don't want to be treated
any way at all.

Every person has his own interpretation of his life.
Unfortunately, most challenged people have a continual
nagging feeling that their disability is showing. People are
staring. Other students are talking about them. They are
sure of that.

In reality, all young people feel that way. But since the
handicapped person has an obvious difference (hearing
aids, for instance), he feels as if a neon sign were blinking
on his body. It is hard to get over that feeling. The
challenged person is overwhelmed by his differences
during his teens. Adult body developments and hormone
changes are turning his life around. He has all he can do to
forget his challenge and carry on an average day.

JENNIFER

I was born with a cleft lip and palate. I've had two
surgical operations to correct everything. Actually, I
look pretty good compared to the pictures when I was
first born. But I feel different. The way I look is okay.
I realize that I don't have a movie star face, but I'm
not ugly. But when I get in the middle of a new group,
like the beginning of a school year, I begin to get those
feelings. The old feelings that everyone is staring at
me, everyone thinks I'm weird because my lips do not
move over my teeth in just the normal way. Then
there are the kids who ignore me altogether because
they think I'm not good enough for them. My mind
knows better. My heart knows that I have friends and
a life I'm happy with most of the time. But those
times, those feelings of extra attention — negative

attention — make my first few weeks of school *very* uncomfortable.

TAKE THE LOVE OF YOU WITH YOU

It's a tough job to hold onto the love and comfortable feelings you have when you're with true friends and family and take them with you to every new situation. That is what you have to strive to do, however. Remember, you know there is a terrific person inside that body of yours, no matter what. Taking the goodness within you and making sure that people see that goodness is a great goal for every day of your life. The trouble is that many "average" people do not have the accepting attitude needed even to get past the outward appearance of a handicapped person. That is where the love of yourself must be plugged in, to shed some light on those unaccepting people. You must teach them about yourself with your kindness and patience.

KEITH

I have cerebral palsy. I was born with it. My body movements are jerky and spastic. Although I tell my limbs to slow down, get controlled, they move every which way. People who don't know me very well can't stand to look at me. First they stare; but when I notice, they quickly look away. Actually, most of the kids in school just turn around and walk the other way. I can't help it, some days that gets me really down in the dumps. Some days I get good and mad. Then I just give up and stare back! I developed that trick, really out of anger, when I was about ten. I got tired of people either running up to me and carrying my stuff for me, or taking a quick critical look and then running away. I began to stare back until *they* were the ones who felt uncomfortable. It was fun! I loved making them feel rotten. But now that I'm in high school, I figure that is not the way to make happy people, or close friends. So I do a variation of my "stare-down," but with modifications. I keep eye contact and start talking about myself. I don't give a sermon or anything. I just start explaining about my body movements. I try to make them comfortable by breaking down this *unknown creature* they see before them. Fortunately, I have very little brain damage, and I have had enough rehabilitation and training to speak with some intelligence. I certainly do not speak as well as I write. But I try to make the other people in my world understand me. Then they begin to get over their uncertainty because they know more about me.

TAKING THE LEAD

The physically challenged person is faced not only with the trials of being visually different, but also with being the teacher of other people. If we as a society, as a group of people living together on one earth, do not learn from each other, differences will divide us. In place of understanding and growth, the challenged will become more alienated. Surely if we would all recognize the sameness of our earthmates, we could begin the understanding process.

The challenged person is best qualified to begin that process toward compassion because he or she is the expert in understanding the situation. The challenges are fully and personally known, and thus he or she is the best teacher to help others learn to know. Tensions mount. People feel uncomfortable. The challenged person can calm those feelings simply by bringing them out in the open. It takes a few sentences of honesty to break the ice.

LYNN

Ever since I was a little girl in preschool, my mother would come in with me and talk to my new classmates about me. I have Down's syndrome. I look different. I speak differently. But I'm smart. My mother and I talk about me to my new classmates every year. We talk and ask questions, and they talk and ask questions. I learn their names, they learn about me. Sometimes I learn about a new handicap, different from mine. I'm nice, and they learn that during Mom's visit. I feel better when everyone knows me. Everyone else feels better too, even my new teachers.

MARK

I have severe asthma. I have trouble breathing a lot of days. I keep the inhaler with me at all times. I'm used to the way I have to live. If I follow the doctor's instructions, listen to my body's signs, and use my medicine, I feel great. But when I am going into an attack I start wheezing and coughing. Then, wherever I am, I leave and go to the restroom to use my inhaler. Guys in the bathroom can hear the medicine being sprayed. They wonder what kind of weird guy I am. I never care about that at the time of an attack, because I'm just glad to do something to help me breathe again. It's when I feel good that I think about others and how they think of me. My father and I have been teaching a Science Unit every March during Science Week at school. He brings in all the different pieces of equipment I've used over my thirteen years of living with asthma. We line up the humidifiers, vaporizers, medicines, many-colored inhalers, breathing machines, and even a tent for my crib. Then we talk. That really helps me feel at ease, and I notice a big change in the people around me after Science Week. I get more hellos in the halls, more smiles. They understand, so they're not afraid of me. Heck, maybe they think I'll drop dead right in front of them one day when I start to wheeze! My coughing spells are fairly loud. Who knows what other people think? I can't mess around worrying about them. Dad and I feel that the best way to make *my* life easier is help others understand asthma. It works. I live my way, people live theirs. If we share how we live, then we all live better lives.

CINDY

I have ataxia. That's a general word for uncontrollable muscle coordination caused by degeneration of the nerves, especially in my legs. What I don't like is people taking over for me. I already feel helpless enough. Since my disease, my entire family does *everything* to make my life easier. That may sound great to you, but it makes me feel like an invalid. That word is defined in the dictionary as: "to remove from active duty by reason of sickness or disability." *In— valid!* Yuck! I do not feel sick at all! I'm a *valid* and very *active* person! I want to fight to remain my cheerleading, tennis-playing self. I don't want my sister to do my chores for me. If I can't do the bathroom sink without my crutches, I'll clean it standing *with* my crutches. Do you understand my point? We handicapped people need to have regular jobs and be treated like human beings with brains and feelings. I do not want to have my books carried for me, or to have my shoes tied for me because it takes double the time to tie them myself. I'll get up earlier to get myself ready, so I can feel more productive, prouder of my personal, inner self. People must understand. They can't walk on eggs around me. My parents haven't yelled at me for anything since my disease started to surface. That's not normal for parents and kids. I don't want to be a spoiled brat; I want to do for myself. If I'm mean to my sister, pick fights, take my disease out on others, I should be yelled at to cooperate the way my parents used to do. I can't stand overhearing others talking about me, trying to be "more understanding" about "my condition." I'm a teenager who wants to date that cute guy in Math class, that's all. I don't want to be treated as if they feel sorry for me. It makes me mad. I have to get control of this and just tell my parents, "Enough is enough."

COMMUNICATION

Communication with loved ones is an extremely important part of dealing with a disability. The people around you cannot read your mind. Also they have their own sadness about seeing you go through difficult times. It is not selfish of them. Loving a challenged person is a challenge all by itself. Communication is the key to releasing all those uneasy feelings. Life is for living *through* experiences, not closing the mouth and keeping quiet.

HOW TO BEGIN COMMUNICATING YOUR FEELINGS

1. Stop and think about the love and caring you have for the person you'd like to talk with. This new

communication should come out of that caring.
The reason to share feelings is to promote goodness, not to make another person feel as bad as you
may feel.

2. Yelling and screaming *are* allowed, provided you
set the stage by saying something like:

"I have these feelings I want to get out in the open.
Then I'd like to talk with you about them. Is this a
good time for you? If not, let's set aside a time right
now."

When that time comes, start out *with love:*

"I care about you. I don't want to lose you. I want
to work out my feelings (my anger, my sadness, my
frustration) with you because you are important to
me."

3. State your feelings as best you can. Don't accuse
people of wrongdoing. Explain it something like
this:
   a) "From my point of view, I see . . . "
   b) "When you do that, my reaction is . . . "
   c) "I get so angry when _____. I know you don't
   mean to hurt me, but that's how I feel. What
   can we do *together* to help us both feel better?"
4. Be prepared to hear things about yourself that
may be less than perfect. When that happens,
don't get on the defensive. Share the sadness that
you may have hurt your loved one. If you want to
be understood, you have to take time to understand others too.
5. Decide together on a new behavior. Every day is a

new day. If you feel awful in a couple of days, have another talk. Forgive the fact that your loved one is not perfect. Forgive yourself for slipping into old ways. Retraining to form a happier life is not easy.

6. Keep your goal right at the front of your mind: You want a better life for yourself. You want the ones you care about to be happy to be with you as well.

BEHAVIOR CHART

Feeling	Appropriate Behavior
Anger	Get out: Take a walk, a ride, or simply leave the room.
	Write it in your diary.
	After a breather, find time to discuss your feelings with someone; the best person to talk with is the person who made you mad.
Sadness	Cry.
	Write down your thoughts.
	Tell someone.
	Be thoughtful toward someone else; it can take sadness away.
Helplessness	Tell someone.
	Write it in your diary.
	Do one small thing you *know* you can do well; enjoy that success. Remember: you *CAN* do *MANY* things.
Joy	Share the moment with someone.
	Write it in your diary so you can reread it during a sad time.
	Hug yourself; pat yourself on the back; drink in your happy feelings.

RESPONSIBILITY FOR YOUR OWN LIFE

Even though it may seem that blaming people is good for you, it has drawbacks. You can always find fault. You can always be angry at something someone has done. Negativity is catching. The healthier way to live with people who act in ways you would rather not see is to discuss with them what's on your mind. This is *your* life. You would like to be happier. *Doing* something toward that happiness, like talking about your thoughts, can change your whole life. When you get your feelings out, understanding and learning will come. Learning through experience is living. Shutting others out is avoiding the life that you've been given to live.

CHAPTER 4

Self-Worth: The Importance of a Positive Self-Image

T he previous chapter told the personal experiences of several physically challenged teenagers. Let's look at the core of each person.

Many suggestions have been made so far on how you can begin to make a better life for yourself, to love the inner you. But how can you tell if you don't love yourself enough? How can you tell if you are depressed or negative about your inner self?

To point out some behaviors, let's look at *Justin*. He wants to be left alone. Is being alone bad or good? It depends on your attitude toward it. Are you feeling that you want to escape? Do you want to avoid situations simply because they make you uncomfortable? That is normal — but only up to a point. If a person continually avoids daily living, not wanting to deal with life's up and down moments, that person needs to work on his or her inner feelings. If, on the other hand, time alone is a chance to think things over, to become ready for the next challenge, then alone-time is a positive time for you.

When you are alone, try some of the more positive behavior/attitudes suggested in this table.

NEGATIVE ALONE-TIME	POSITIVE ALONE-TIME
Going to your room to hide.	a) Rest, breathe slowly, try to relax. b) Think about why you want to hide. c) Write down some of your thoughts — one-word descriptions or lengthy sentences, depending on how you feel.
Turning away when someone asks or says things that make you uncomfortable.	Don't hold your thoughts in. Tell the person how the things he is doing or saying bother you, or no one will know what is the matter.
Ignoring or not answering when someone speaks to you in a way you do not like or stares at you.	Say what is on your mind: a) "I don't want to discuss that right now." b) "Okay, since you seem interested, I'll explain my situation a little." c) "I'm afraid to talk to you because I do not want to be made fun of." *Stare back.* Say, "Staring makes people feel awful, doesn't it?"

LETTING OUT YOUR INNER SELF

Who can get to know and like you if you never tell anyone your thoughts? Who will know the whole thought behind your eyes when you tell only part of it? How can *you* know what is inside you, how you're developing and growing up, if you don't discuss your thoughts and feelings with people? You can either remain a secret and grow up very little or begin to share your *self.*

Look back at *Lynn* and *Mark* for a minute. They feel much more comfortable and happy when their parents take time to explain their handicaps to their classmates. They take time to care, and the new classmates end up caring in return. People give back what they get. Don't be angry all the time, *explain* to a friend that you're angry. If you treat people negatively, you'll get negative treatment in return, and that is just what you don't want.

If you show people that you are a regular human being, many of your classmates and new friends will begin to treat you like one.

THE RUDE PEOPLE

Consider *Jennifer*'s and *Keith*'s comments. The negative, "making fun" people are the ones that really bother them. How can you change those people? How can you stop them? There are two ways. First, try to be strong and hang in through the uneasy feelings long enough to get in a few words about what your life is like. Second, if they don't listen, forget it for the moment and teach them about yourself another time. Perhaps another day they'll be more likely to listen.

Keith had the right idea: The unknown is scary to most people. If you want to be friends, let yourself out of your shell, explain what your life is like. Eventually word will get around. Listeners will tell other listeners, and gradually people will even talk to you *about you.* Perhaps they'll ask questions. That's how friendships begin. If you get a few understanding friends on your side, the rude people come off looking really mean. You've led your new friends to a new point of view.

KNOWING YOURSELF

Every person on earth is in the process of learning to know him or herself. It is a lifelong task. Billions of people share this planet with us. Use some of them to learn from and bounce ideas around with. Write down your feelings and thoughts. *Think* when you're full of emotion. If you can explain how you feel to yourself, as *Cindy* does, you can begin to communicate with others. Forming our own selves takes time and work. Whether we like it or not, we can't read each other's minds — yet. Talking, commenting, and verbalizing are important talents to develop. These communication skills take a lifetime to perfect. Begin now, so that you don't feel alone.

YOU'LL ALWAYS HAVE YOU

What if you are a quiet person? What if you don't usually feel like explaining your handicap to anyone? Is that bad?

SETH

At seventeen I've finally figured it out: I'm basically a loner. I love reading. I look things up, research things. I keep interesting information in my own two-drawer filing cabinet. I know more about hemophilia than any senior in my 900–student class. It's my disease. I bleed and can't stop sometimes. But you know, on an average day I don't even think about my disease. I have two best friends. That's all. I don't need any more. When they're not with me, I just do my own stuff. They understand me. I don't have to be bothered explaining myself over and over. I know my buddies like me. I really like them too. Our being friends has helped me learn that I'm a great guy in my own way. Now, even when I'm by myself, I'm happy.

BE GOOD TO YOURSELF

No matter who, no matter what, you can always count on yourself. Be good to yourself. Be proud of your accomplishments. Work hard to succeed in other things. Have friends. You don't have to have a million of them, but it is important to share life with others. If your favorite people are not available, you can do one of two things: Use the time to be alone happily doing what you love to do; or try reaching out to someone else for a change. The effort you make can become a gift to yourself: a new friend.

Be happy being alone. Be happy sharing yourself. Rely on yourself with or without others. You can be satisfied with both "yous."

CHAPTER ◇ 5

Personal Independence and Friends, Too

ROB

I feel the way Cindy does. I want to do things for myself and be respected by my family and friends. I'm a paraplegic; I need a wheelchair to get around. When my friends first heard about my car accident, they even did my homework for me. It's not that I'm not grateful. I am. But after a while I got to feeling like a king. Then when my friends were busy and unable to visit, I went into a real depression. I cried and cried in my room. "Nobody likes me anymore," I thought. I hated my life. "How am I ever going to live without everyone doing my stuff for me?", I used to lie awake thinking.

My parents took me to a counselor for people going

through traumatic experiences like losing a part of you. Slowly, the counselor set goals for me to do every week. Then I began to choose the goals with him. Now I plan my own goals. It makes me feel good inside to know that I am able. Let me show you a chart we made up. I used to put a check by the things I did, then show the chart to my counselor the following week. Now I call it my "Feel Good Chart" because that's how it makes me feel: *Good*!

THE FEEL GOOD CHART

	Make bed	Brush teeth	Walk on crutches	Make dinner	Be kind to my brother	Call a friend
Monday						
Tuesday						
Wednesday						
Thursday						
Friday						
Saturday						
Sunday						

FEELING INDEPENDENT AND FREE

Rob feels good about himself because he has gone beyond the stage of dependence on others to relying on himself and his abilities. Rob now considers the counselor's charts his own charts of success. If you feel that you don't have enough freedom from your disability, perhaps a "Feel Good Chart" is for you. Make one up and give it a couple of weeks. Put any goals you want to accomplish on the top line. See how many things you can do every day of the week. You could put a chart right in your diary if you like. Or you and your parents could try it together if you need help on some of your goals. You will be surprised at how many things you are *ABLE* to do. Showing your plans to your family and friends can win their respect. You are a person who is trying to do for yourself, trying to be strong from within *you*.

HOW TO BE A GOOD FRIEND

Many physically challenged persons have the experience that Cindy and Rob have had. The people who care for them start doing everything for them. A person can get spoiled (pay attention to that word *spoiled*: not good any more) into thinking things will be done for him or her forever. Let's face it, you're the disabled one; you need all the sympathy and gifts you can get to make you feel better, right? Wrong! Others have to live their lives, too. You can't expect to receive without giving, no matter how many people do things for you. Another person cannot live your life for you. Someday you'll want to live apart from your family. Then what? If you don't start to do for yourself while there are people around to lend a hand, you'll be stuck not knowing how to do much. And your friends will eventually want to live their own lives; they're not getting much of a friendship from you. You can't blame them for wanting a give-and-take friendship with others. They have to replenish themselves with people who give back.

You cannot expect to continue to use people and their energies. They will get tired. They will have to stop seeing you, have to stop doing your homework for you. One day they won't be able to take your grumpiness. They just won't come back. What will you do?

You must be a friend back. You must show kindness and caring to your family and friends. You cannot take and take. You must *be* a friend to have one. How can you do all that with your disability staring you in the face every morning?

1. Try Rob's chart. Accomplish something.
2. Learn to love yourself *again*.
3. Give love back that so your family and friends have a new supply.
4. Expect to be a friend if you have one.
5. Be thankful you *are able* to do many things.
6. You *can* be a wonderful friend — *now*.

CHAPTER 6

Peers, Adolescent Changes, and Dating

JULIE

My hair never stays right. I have pimples now. I never had a single one before my first period two years ago. My growing breasts are making my favorite clothes look like they don't fit at all. To top it off, I was born dyslexic. I have a terrible time learning from books in school. I go to special classes and do a lot of extra studying. I feel like a mess. Some days I think I'm going crazy because I like this one boy in my class so much. How can I make him like me when I don't like much about myself?

EVERY TEEN FEELS OFF BALANCE AT TIMES

Not one person is perfect. Not one human even *feels* perfect. Something always seems to need improvement. Why should it be a surprise to read about a very normal teen like Julie? Adolescence is a jumbled time. Adding an extra handicap to a young person's life is a setup for frustration.

CLING TO THOSE WHO LOVE YOU

Young people should turn to their family members and established friends. The teens are years of continual change. When a teen needs to find a homebase of stability, she must look close by. The people who love her can make her feel stable, more sure. Real love doesn't change, even though the adolescent is overwhelmed with change.

Independent thought, hormonal changes, striving to become an adult are all part of normal teen years. But the physically challenged teenager has more than she can handle at times with her added challenges. Disabilities become larger than they need be: burdens that seem too heavy to bear when coupled with the normal changes of puberty. During these difficult times a counselor, psychologist, or other medical professional can be of help to the handicapped person and her family.

WAYS TO COPE WITH PEERS
AND DATING

1. To promote peer understanding, arrange gatherings at the disabled person's home once in a while. It could be an hour or two after school or a Saturday. Make a point of discussing feelings and troubles; even touch on handicaps and coping day to day.

2. During a medical visit, ask about a young people's support group. Go to a few meetings. Give the group a solid chance. There is often comfort in the company of agemates in the same dilemma.

3. Join a brand-new (to you) school or church youth group. Chances to get to know classmates in a group are easier than going on a date with someone you "think" you like. Trips and activities often give young people an opportunity to become friends simply by being and working together.

4. Be in charge of a lesson on your particular challenge. Suggest to your teacher that you are interested in being a guest speaker or demonstrator for your class. Bring a brother, sister, cousin, or parent if you don't want to do it alone. Make the lesson interesting. If you use special tools or equipment to help with your handicap, bring all that along. This approach promotes understanding. Understanding each other is the path to friendship. Friendship is the best basis for dating.

5. Look to your trusted friends for dating or going places. A comfortable relationship can turn a dance into a wonderful experience. Set yourself up for a successful, enjoyable time.

6. Know in your heart that you'll be fine. You already have people in your life who love you. Communicate with them if a new relationship doesn't go the way you like.

7. Do not do something you are not comfortable with just to foster a relationship. Disabled people can seem easy to take advantage of. Know what you want and *don't want*. Go home if things are not going the way you like. Love yourself enough to make sure you are treated well.

MELODY

I am legally blind. I was born that way. I can see shadows but cannot make out detail or colors. I'm nineteen now. When I was seventeen I was almost raped. I went out on a date with a guy I had just met where I worked. It seemed like a great idea at the time, just a movie. He came to the house, met my parents, drove a nice car. Because I'm blind, I expected to be understood and helped along a little. He started touching me when I didn't even know he was going to. I was scared. I told him I needed to go to the bathroom. He took me to the door of the ladies room, and I asked a girl there to call my family. I stayed in the ladies room until Mom came. I didn't care what that guy thought I was doing in that ladies room; I was going to stay safe.

I'm proud of myself for knowing how to get out of a situation that I hated. Now, I tend to date in groups or with another couple until I really know the guy. I never want to be in that position again.

DATING WITH INTELLIGENCE

The realities of dating can be much more than the physically challenged teen was aware of when she casually said, "Sure, I'd love to go to the movies with you." Reality is harsh and sometimes cruel. The dating approach Melody finally chose is a safe one. Know your partner before going anywhere with him alone. The disabled person is at a disadvantage when she cannot fend for herself. She is somewhat dependent on the partner to treat her with understanding. That may not happen if she dates someone she doesn't know well. Think. There is no need to become paranoid about dating. If you know your date, there is little to fear. Be independent with your choices, so that when you need someone he will be understanding enough to be there for you. A true friend has your interests in mind, not just his. Every date should be a meeting of two minds, not a one-way street where you have no control.

JOSHUA

I have had a very hard time dating. I was born with spina bifida. I've had operations to close and heal my spine, but I can't walk. I need my wheelchair. But I wish I didn't when I want to ask a new girl out. I try, believe me. I was lucky that a group at our church saved up money to help my parents buy me a car with hand controls. So a car isn't the problem. It's my being able to get out of the car and go into a movie or restaurant that takes a lot of patience from my date. I can manage to get out of the car and everything, but it takes time. A lot of the girls I ask out get an impatient look in their eyes, or they look around because they're embarrassed to be seen with me. I wish they'd forget other people and get to know me. I'm a kind, nice guy.

Now that I'm turning eighteen next week, I've decided to do what Melody does: go out with my buddies and their girls, or at least with one other couple. That keeps things lively and gives me time to get myself organized in my wheelchair and up to the door of my choice of entertainment. I love women, but not that many of them seem to like me — as a boyfriend, that is. That makes me feel pretty low sometimes, but my best friends cheer me up. I know whoever I end up marrying will have to have a lot of understanding and patience. I just haven't found my girl yet, that's all.

CHAPTER ◇ 7

Adaptation:
Everyday Frustrations

Adolescence is frustration. For the average young adult days and days go by filled with self-doubt and self-considered failures. A D on a report because of a misunderstanding can catapult a person into a series of nightmarish daydreams about what a nonsuccess he is. Losing means total disaster. Not being chosen makes the insecure young person feel an outcast for life. Things are either black or white. Life becomes a succession of highs and lows. Accomplishment versus devastation is the war inside the teen.

Doubly affected by all these striving-to-be-an-adult experiences is the physically challenged youth. He is feeling not only the tremendous hormonal surges of growth, but also the uncertainties and unchangeable certainties of his disability.

Daily existence is often overwhelming. Professional medical and psychological help can be very useful in providing extra guidance for working through these days.

Adolescence itself can be an excellent reason for seeking counseling for the entire family. Counseling for the disabled adolescent seems highly appropriate when life becomes out of control.

JOSEPH

I lost an eye in a hunting accident. I used to wear a patch until my glass eye was fitted properly. Now my prosthetic eye looks pretty good. When I look at myself in the mirror it's a lot better than without the glass eye, but inside I feel almost blind. Inside I feel that every single person in school, in the mall, or even in a dark movie theatre *is staring at me*! Lately I can't bear to go anywhere. My mother says I will get used to living with one eye. My father, who doesn't live with us, never says anything one way or the other. Me, I just *hate* losing my eye.

ALL HUMANS ARE IN THE SAME CONDITION

As Dr. Leo Buscaglia says in his book, *Living, Loving, and Learning*, "We're all brailling the world . . . I am becoming, for in reality, in so many ways, we are not even born yet . . ."

Children are the freshest forms of the life experience. Adolescents have an added mix-me-up of "hormonal imbalance and balancing" blending into their almost new lives. Adults are supposed to be all "grown up" but find every day filled with more learning than the day before. What does this mean?

People of all ages are trying to find out how they feel and think about the thing called *Life*. If we could only remember how each stage feels, or try to understand the other fellow's point of view, we would be more at peace with our own learning curve.

THE LEARNING CURVE

Personal learning *is* a curve. It has no particular beginning. It has no end. People — children, teens, and adults — all learn at their own speed. The pace of a person's learning means little. It is what is learned that is the wealth of life called knowledge and wisdom.

Disabled people may or may not be slower at learning. They must be given the chance to learn, however, whichever way they are able.

Many things depend on how the teen can get along physically. Joseph, for instance, says he is doing well. But he seems to have slowed the growth of his learning because he is very busy *hating* where he is. As stated in Chapter 2, the grief process first described by Dr. Elisabeth Kubler-Ross is a normal one. It is when a person becomes slowed down or stuck that the mind does not grow as well. So the mental image of a curve of learning can very clearly illustrate where you are in learning if you think of your life as a curve of continual experiences.

LIFE-CURVE OF LEARNING

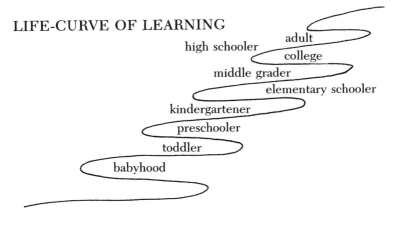

adult
high schooler
college
middle grader
elementary schooler
kindergartener
preschooler
toddler
babyhood

TAKE TIME TO THINK

Take a day or two to think about this basic curve. Think about Joseph, if it will help you get used to the idea of putting names on different parts of your life. He was an average two-eyed human, born a baby. He progressed, probably without realizing it, until the day of his hunting accident and the loss of his eye at age fifteen. There, as illustrated below, Joseph slowed down. He seems to be a bit stuck on his curve of life learning. There is little movement, little growth.

JOSEPH'S LIFE-CURVE OF LEARNING

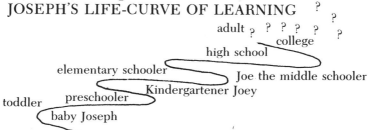

CAN A PERSON BE STUCK AND NOT REALIZE IT?

Often the grief or loss process can get stuck without the person even realizing that he is "treading water." How can you tell if you're stuck? Think. Think back to the last time you can say you really learned something *important* — not important to anyone else, but *something important to you.*

The difficulty physically challenged people can run into is having to deal with their disability day in and day out. Joseph's eye cannot see. It lost its ability to see yesterdays ago. He cannot see out of it today. He will not see out of it tomorrow. That is the problem with the physicalness of being disabled. The person can learn about his challenge. He can read about his challenge. He can talk about his challenge. He can even decide to have operations to change his challenge. But often the challenge *remains*. The *physical challenge remains*.

OUR MAPS OF LIFE

Thinking in terms of the Life-Curve can help you understand where you are on the map of your life. The purpose of life, as most people agree, is to make your journey a loving, wonderful, fun path of growth. As M. Scott Peck, MD, says in his book *The Road Less Traveled*: "The Outdated Map . . . The process of active clinging to an outmoded view of reality is the basis for much mental illness. Psychiatrists refer to it as transference . . . " Dr. Peck points out that the old way of thinking cannot apply as you grow. Growth is change, no matter how much we all seem to want to keep things the same.

Of course, disabled people are not all mentally ill. Not all people going through change are bound to get stuck. But it happens at times. If these times of your life seem very long, almost too long — then change! You have the power to think differently. Look at your list of things you need to get at the mental health store. Go shopping often, because health is always needed. You have the keys:

1. Decide on the things you can and cannot change in your life. Make a list like the following:

Cannot Change	Can change
• Your *basic* body: head size, toes, heart, blood, missing limbs, nonwalking legs, etc.	The *condition* of your body: eat better, exercise, do physical therapy.
• Your parents, your family.	How you view your family; your attitude.
• You have to go to school.	What you *decide* to do with all the time you have to spend in school.

2. Take one item you can change and make it your goal. Make a list of ways you can make that part of your journey a happier, healthier one.

ERIC

I hate school. Kids are always staring at me. They distract me, and I get poor grades. Poor grades make me feel like a total failure. My parents say they *know* I can do better. How do they know that? They don't tell me how I can do better except *study, study, study,* and that makes me hate school even more.

3. Change your mind. Decide to find something that you like about the challenges in your life. Think about that happy part of your life all day. *Do not* let any one thing or person change your mind. *Know* that this part of your life is a special happy part. It's *your* happiness.

EXAMPLE:

Let's understand Eric's situation and use #3 to help him make his day a pleasant journey. He hates school for such reasons as, "Kids are always staring at me," and "They distract me." Does that mean that he honestly hates school? It seems as if he hates kids staring at him. That one dislike makes all the dominoes lined up in his day fall one by one. How can he change that? He can't change anyone. He *can* change his ideas about staring. He can simply decide that he doesn't care where people look, he's going to enjoy his classwork and the friends who do understand him. He can go to school for the next week and try not to waste time thinking about where people are looking. He can realize that he actually stares at people and things sometimes, too. As he keeps thinking, "Don't waste your time. Think about something you like," he can slowly come to see that he has more time to pay attention to his teacher. The next classes can be fun because he is paying attention instead of fighting the old thoughts of how people are looking at him. "People look around them all the time. So what! Big deal! They cannot hurt me if I choose to pay attention to something else." Eric will see a change in his grades if he keeps this line of new thinking going!

4. Continue making little lists of things you would like to change about your life. You have to be patient with yourself. New thinking does take work. But all the energy you're *not using* on your old way of thinking can go to the new thought of the day. If you feel sad again, that's okay. Take a break. After school take an hour and forget your new thinking. Travel your life's map tomorrow if things are not falling into place today. The big point is that you are working on your learning curve again. Just *trying* counts, too. And remember, the situation may be *awful* to you, but your thinking *can be what you want.*

THE TRYING IS THE GROWING

The very fact that you are reading and trying to learn from this book shows that you are working toward a happier life. That is terrific! Don't forget to hug yourself. You could even share a hug with someone else, too!

CHAPTER ◇ 8

Sorrow

SARAH

Most of my life is sad. I keep trying to do things to make me happy, but those things don't keep me happy for very long. I was bitten all over the face by a dog when I was only two. All my life I have been trying to forget that. But every time I look in a mirror, or even catch a glimpse in a store window, my insides flip a little. It's like a nest of butterflies never settling down inside me. When I have a really sad week feeling bad about my life, I actually throw up every morning. I have had plastic surgeries, but a lot of scars are still there, on the outside and within. All the years I've been alive, all I seem to be able to remember is my sadness. I wonder when my life will get better?

Sorrow and sadness are the other sides of joy and happiness. Without them, we would not be able to compare and know how happy we *can* be.

Sarah has not figured out too many happinesses yet, has she? What could we do as caring people to help a friend like Sarah? Could a friend *make* her happy? Is it our job to go around *making* people happy?

The best thing we could do for Sarah would be to show her how to find her own daily joys. She needs a helping hand. Maybe she needs a counselor. Perhaps the school guidance people could help her, too.

To begin with, however, let's talk it out with Sarah. Let's see if she thinks she has a problem she can fix.

Friend/ Counselor:	"Do you like life? What is a favorite part of your day?"
Sarah:	"I like being a cheerleader because I love sports and people in the stands can't see my scars from so far away."
Friend/ Counselor:	"Okay, I'm glad to hear you like cheer-leading. Is there another reason for liking it besides being far away from people?"
Sarah:	"Yes, I love to do gymnastic-type things. I have been taking exercise classes all my life. I even won an award in a gymnastics competition!"
F:	"Great! Are there any other things you feel good about on the days you don't cheer?"
S:	"Well, I guess I'm a pretty good student. I made the Honor Roll last report period. I'd like to end my junior year with High Honors, but nothing like that has ever happened to me before."
F:	"What do you think you could do to make sure you get on the High Honor Roll?"
S:	"Well, if I gave up one TV show a night and used that extra time to go over all my notes and reread my assignments and

	stuff, I guess I couldn't miss. I mean, I'm already on the Honor Roll . . ."
F:	"Why don't you try it for two weeks and see if your marks improve? That would give you a good idea whether your plan could work or not, way before the end of the marking period."
S:	"Well, I suppose I could try it. I want to go to college and learn to help children, so I should get the best grades I can right now . . ."
F:	"Great! I'll talk to you in a couple of weeks to see how your idea worked."

SEEING THE BIG PICTURE

To follow the line of thinking illustrated above, let's discuss why the friend/counselor asked the kind of questions she did and what we might understand about Sarah from her replies.

1. Sarah does not seem to be entirely depressed, as she was able to cite a happy experience that she enjoys regularly: cheerleading. It is important to *listen*. A very sad person can be on the brink of suicide if you cannot get any positive responses from her. It is important to seek professional help to try to bring a friend or relative out of continual sadness. Frequently, a friend is the best person to understand the severity of a person's sorrow. Get help. Don't give up on a person you care for. Share the problem with a person trained to help.

2. The friend asked only questions that would lead Sarah to pleasing thoughts. That can help a person see the light at a time of darkness.

3. The friend's questions tried to lead Sarah to realize that her everyday life did have some happy and positive moments. A sign of Sarah's basic good health is that she sees her potential for being an even better student than she is. The key point is that she already realizes she has done well at *something*. The good counselor/friend will always support this wonderful attitude and try to see it grow *bigger* and *better*.

4. The friend tried to lead Sarah (by repeating her own positive words) into planning a very attainable goal in the *near future*. That is extremely important in dealing with sorrow. The sad person needs to set a short-term goal important to her "self" and see that goal as easily reached by planning. The plans must be broken down into small daily steps. The process must be followed up by a caring person (at least at the beginning). Then a celebration and acceptance of success must occur to encourage the person on to the next goal.

5. Following through soon with another discussion of the plan assures the person that she has someone to lean on. That is not a forever commitment, but a helping hand for a limited time until the friend/ counselor can see the sadness lifted and a few more goals attained.

6. The end result of this approach is that the depressed person becomes more self-motivated and happy. We all need friends and loved ones to help share our happiness, but inner joy must be self-started. Otherwise we will always be sad if another person is not there to "make us happy." Each and every person has to decide to create her own joy. Then any extra we receive from and

through others is an added bonus. With that approach, there is always something to smile about!

JAKE

I can't do anything right. I was drinking and driving last year and totaled my car and broke my back. I can't walk now. Heck, I should have known better. I mean, any idiot can see the TV commercials on drinking and driving deaths. Still I did it. Now look at me. I'm a waste. My girlfriend doesn't even want to go out anymore. I can never take gym, let alone be center forward on the varsity basketball team. This isn't a life; it's a death sentence.

In *Coping with Death*, Dr. Robert Raab writes: "Suicide is a form of self-punishment." When a person feels so guilty about what has happened in his life, it is extremely serious. Feeling guilt can cause deep depression. Often the overwhelmingly depressed person sees no way out of his situation. If he does not see a way out, set a goal and attain it, and then set other goals and grow through *and past* his stress, he can fall into a deeper depression. Death can seem the only way out. Jake feels so awful, so guilty, that he could think he deserves to die. He is so sick with sorrow over his mistake that he may choose suicide as his only way out. At all costs, Jake's cry for help must be answered.

DO NOT TRY TO LIVE ANOTHER PERSON'S LIFE

Know that sorrow is an extremely strong emotion. It can make people like Sarah physically ill to the point of vomiting. The depths of depression could cause Jake to kill himself. We have ears, as human beings. Ears are for listening to our fellow man. If you hear a friend or relative cry out, give him a hand that will lead him to a better attitude. If you see someone in trouble, seek advice from a trusted person in your life. If you do not get fast action, try another trusted friend. Try to follow through until the person in sorrow is in good, trained hands that will guide him or her to a healthier mind.

HOW IS YOUR ATTITUDE?

Now that you have seen two examples of sorrow, think about your own inner feelings. Do some of the comments by Sarah or Jake sound like thoughts you have had or are continually having? Are you so unhappy that you cannot point out anything *today* that could make you smile? Think. Become aware of your inner *you*. Take care of you. Share some of your darkest thoughts about your life with another person. Often, simply talking out a feeling can release it from inside you forever. Sometimes crying is an excellent tool for letting go of sorrow. Do not listen to anyone who tells you not to cry. If you feel like having a cry, or if you cry spontaneously, allow yourself the cleansing value this precious behavior can give. Often exhausting, a good cry can result in a nap and then an awakening to a fresh start on your journey through life!

YOUR JOURNEY INWARD

Whatever you find as you look into your heart and soul, try to rethink one sadness. Talk it out, write it out in your journal, try to think of a way to change even a small part of your sadness into a joy. That is the key to inner happiness: finding *your* own way to turn *your* thoughts around.

Not surprisingly, books on death are good sources of informaion on sorrow. If more information on depression is what you seek, perhaps reading a book specifically about death will give you new understanding of your feelings of sadness. Sometimes books on death can actually make you appreciate the wonderful things about your life. It is a good idea to explain to your parents or relatives why you are reading a book on death. Often people think such books are depressing unto themselves. If someone asks you, "Why are you reading a book on death?" you can simply reply that you want to understand sorrowful emotions better. You feel sad and would like to know more about it. Beware! A healthy conversation involving the sharing of feelings may follow!

CHAPTER 9

A Partnership with Medical Personnel

The matter of medical professionals is frequently a sore subject for the physically challenged young adult. In this age of medical breakthroughs the disabled child born within the past twenty to thirty years has in all likelihood had some form of intense medical follow-up.

Of course, all the medical fields have advanced to solve many problems faced by babies born with special needs and challenges. Several opportunities often exist for the accident or disease victim as well.

But to the baby, medical people in white are sources of pokes, prods, and regular pains in their little necks. Even entering a hospital or rehabilitation center can cause the baby to sniff the air and cry its little heart out.

To the disabled preschooler, life at the doctor's office is not "Sesame Street." Sure, they have a playroom. Sure, there are cookies and juice. But there are still those cold, metal things hanging from those white-coated necks. Boy, are they like ice when they touch your naked body. Yes, naked. No matter what they want to look at — a toe, for instance — they have to have you naked or in a nightie without a back.

To the middle-schooler, medical people become the *enemy*. Thoughts of an upcoming medical visit usually create vivid nightmares of white-coated people smiling as they make you lie naked (yes, naked) on a freezing-cold *metal* table to take a series of "pictures of your body" that takes five million hours, through two mealtimes. The preteen is *never* interested in disrobing to show anyone her newly formed breasts.

To the young adult, life at medical institutions has become a way of life.

PATRICIA

Sure, I've had operations to try to correct my scoliosis. Sure, I can walk and run now while standing straight up. I am thankful that I live in the twentieth century. At eighteen years of age in colonial times, I would already have been walking almost doubled over because of the curvature of the spine that I was born with. I'm thrilled not be to living that way. I am happy to know the exercises I do every day that keep my spine straight. But the awfully painful things I've had to go through to get where I am . . . Surgery is *not* a date at the movies. I mean, no refreshments were served for days after *my* surgeries, I was so sick to my stomach. Every time I hear my mother or father say that we have an appointment at the clinic, my stomach starts rolling over. I don't know whether I'll ever get used to seeing doctors and therapists, no matter how nice they are.

MODERN MEDICAL SCIENCE

Those are the monthly, often weekly, stresses of using modern science to get along better in life. Disabled young people go through a lot of fear and anxiety because they feel that they have to give up their bodies for others to help them be better. Let's face it, not one person enjoys undressing to be examined by anyone. Our bodies are so private. In reality, of course, only one or two people actually see you without your clothes on, and that only for a few minutes. They usually let you hold some form of fabric over some part of your body. They hardly ever just rush into the room and throw that open-back robe off your shivering body. Actually, compared to the hours you sit in a waiting room, the times when you're naked are fairly brief.

SYMPATHETIC UNDERSTANDING

You have to sympathize with the disabled young person who has to make visits to the doctor and other medical professionals a regular part of life. Often the teenager is bothered by visits to this or that therapist countless times while she is still very young, or just hurt and oh-so-vulnerable. To go and hide, rather than display her body, is what the young person really wants to do. And yet parents and other caretakers of handicapped young people *must* seek help. They *must* let the baby cry in efforts to help the challenged child have the best life possible. It is an extremely uncomfortable position for relatives and friends to be in with a sweet, loving handicapped child.

THE PATH OUT OF NEGATIVE THOUGHT PATTERNS

How can Patricia ever get used to visiting her medical team?

Are medical people the ENEMY?

What is really behind the upset stomachs of patients who must see medical people weekly and monthly?

Feelings of grief are behind those negative reactions.

Let's understand Patricia. She says she is grateful and thankful for living now. That is an excellent attitude. But in her short life of eighteen years she and her family have chosen a course of surgery to help correct her spine. She has had a lot of pain. That is sad. It can bring heartache and depression. She sees her life as better than it would have been, but she is still suffering and grieving inside. And she is putting those ugly, sickening feelings onto all the medical people she sees. After all, she thinks: *"They caused my pain."*

Did they?

"They deserve to see my ugly feelings."

Do they?

"I hate them for being so nice; they really only want to hurt me."

They do?

Think.

JENNY, THE ONCOLOGICAL NURSE

I have chosen a job that most people would never consider: nursing cancer patients. I'm the one who gives the chemotherapy. I chose this profession because my mother had cancer and she hated the way she was treated when she went for chemo every three to five days. I was in high school at the time, and I agreed with her. I used to drive her to the doctor's and hold her hand while she got the medication that helped her become the healthy, active kindergarten teacher she is today. It was true. The office people never asked how she felt, just where is your payment? The nurse who gave her chemo never even talked to us — just jabbed the needle in and walked out while we watched in fearful silence as the sickening medicine dripped. It was awful.

That's why I decided that as a nurse I would do an excellent job of taking care of cancer patients. But it is a tough job. People are so angry about their disease that they grumble, snap, and shout at me. Some days if I can't get one person to smile, I go home and cry! I try to point out happy things to the patients, asking them questions about their families and all. But they are so sad about their lives while they're going through the cancer experience that they can't see *any* joy. But I'll keep trying. Some days I get the whole waiting room full of patients laughing by bringing in my dog to do tricks. Those days when laughter sneaks in make up for the darker days.

TWO SIDES TO EVERY STORY

Of course, there are always other points of view about an experience than just your own. How can we turn around this dismal picture of medical people and patients as enemies?

Let's understand the background of why medical people and patients seem at odds. In the distant past few people were as well educated as the doctors. Gradually medical science became so complex that now a physician spends about a decade of his or her life training to practice medicine. Along the way, medicine began to help prolong lives and sometimes even cure people. Common illnesses have been all but wiped out by vaccines. The life expectancy of a human being is approaching 100 years. It's a little like magic. From this history has evolved a relationship of a godlike person treating the not-so-well-educated patient, a habit of blind trust in the doctor. After all, if I do exactly what he says, I might live longer; I might even be cured.

Doctors and nurses are people. They can make mistakes and bad judgment calls just like every other person. We can trust them, but we should think for ourselves too.

MEDICAL TREATMENT AS A PARTNERSHIP

How can you use the education and expertise of the medical people in your life and still keep some control over your naked body? You have to think of all the medical people working on your case as a team. Think of it as a baseball team. Every single team member is important. But guess what? *You* are the pitcher! *You* have the ball because it's *your* body everyone is rooting for.

Change your mind a little. Yes, the doctor knows more about human bodies and their parts than you do. But you are the expert on you. You've known yourself for years, day in and day out. You know how you feel. Not one doctor can know you as well as you do. If you really pay attention, you can educate yourself even more about your body and how it works. Listen to what your body tells you. Know when you've had enough. Take a break. Know when you're feeling good and go ahead and press forward. Our bodies are wonderful. The only way we can get the most out of life is to listen to our bodies and try very hard to meet their needs. Then after learning from your body, you must learn to communicate that knowledge to your medical team so that they can best help you.

HOW TO BECOME A MEDICAL TEAM PLAYER

1. Listen to your body. What hurts, what's different, what feels great? Tired? Sleep! Overweight? Watch the calories! Weak? Exercise, slowly at first, but do it!
2. Understand that every medical person is a person. He or she has a family, a job, and even gets sick sometimes.
3. Learn about your condition, your handicap in life. Read. Study. Become an expert on your disease, your challenge. You will understand the doctors better and gain a sense of understanding and control of your case and your life.
4. Write questions in a special notebook you take with you every time you visit the doctor or clinic or rehabilitation center. Remember to ask the questions, and write down the answers so that you can refer to them at home. Often a visit to a medical facility is confusing, and this keeps things clear.
5. When you have become good at asking questions, be sure to tell the medical people how you feel about certain things. If a new procedure hurts, yell out! Say so if a new piece of equipment, such as a brace or prosthesis, does not feel just right. Explain what is wrong so they can try to fix it.

These medical people, like Jenny, are there to help you have a better life, but they cannot read your mind. Get a problem solved fast by talking it out right away.

6. After a while, if someone on your medical team is not cooperative when you ask questions, consider getting another team member. *You* are the boss. *You* and your family are the ones who have to live with what the team does. When you spend a lot of time with people, trying to understand and get along, you can expect them to listen and try to understand you. If that is not happening, ask questions, point out the problem to a trusted member of the team, and see to it that you don't have to go through any more unpleasant experiences. You're the one trying to get help; you don't have to take poor treatment.

7. If you find yourself firing your medical team, learn from the experience. Go shopping for another doctor. Ask specific questions about the way he or she treats people like you. Don't be afraid to go to more than one doctor. That is a sign of a smart person, an educated person. If a doctor does not like you getting second opinions, you need to fire him or her too! There is no time in your life for people who do not treat you well and with respect, no matter what your age.

8. *COOPERATE!* Follow the prescribed medications, diets, exercises, and other orders of the team you have chosen. Thinking and asking questions does not mean skipping instructions and doctoring yourself. Remember that you are on a team: All of you must do your best to make

your life the best it can be. Try to trust the people you have chosen. No need to complain all the time unless your life takes a clear turn for the worse.

9. Think of a visit with your medical team as a chance to learn as well as a time-out. Perhaps you can have a special breakfast or lunch before or after your appointment. Turn the day into an outing with the person who goes with you. A day out of school can be a breath of fresh air. Discuss your questions over a frozen yogurt shake or some other treat. You deserve it!

10. Try to think of your office or clinic visits as chances to meet other people with similar challenges. Waiting rooms can be places to learn and make new friends. Ask someone interesting-looking if they've ever had one of the problems you've come across. Try!

Bernie S. Siegel, M.D., author of *Love, Medicine and Miracles*, bases his "healing partnership" philosophy on the cancer research and cancer patients in his practice. But his thoughts are real and practical for all people who need to see medical people on a regular basis:

"Open-mindedness is the hallmark of all physicians who are interested in helping their patients . . . Participation in the decision-making process, more than any other factor, determines the quality of the patient-doctor relationship. The exceptional patient wants to share responsibility for life and treatment, and doctors who encourage that attitude can help their patients heal faster . . ."

IT'S YOUR BODY, YOUR LIFE

Take an interest in your health and your treatment, and you'll feel more in control. Babies lie back and let Mom change them; young adults do more.

CHAPTER 10

Fear and Anger:
The AIDS Crisis

W hy me? Why now? I don't deserve this! I've been a good person, why me?

Hemophiliacs are born missing the clotting factor that stops bleeding. A person with hemophilia who suffers a prolonged blood loss requires a blood transfusion to replenish his body. Ryan White contracted the immune system disease AIDS through a blood transfusion. He died in 1990 and was an exemplar of the philosophy of this book: Do what you can with what you've been given.

If we could choose people who have a right to be angry all the time, one of those people would have been Ryan White. Acquiring a deadly disease while being treated for another disease almost as deadly is the stuff Shakespeare could have written about: the human tragedy of tragedies.

AIDS is affecting our entire world. Babies are being born with it. These babies cannot fight disease; they can die from one little germ. We can stay angry at our own challenges, or we can find a way to use our angry energy in useful ways.

HEROES

All of us need people in our lives to look up to and emulate. In many religions, the image of a Son of God in human form, perfect in every way, is a Hero of Heroes to aspire toward.

But in our everyday lives we need people whom we see daily or fairly often who are living examples of what we would like to become. Setting goals is a marvelous exercise in mental health. If we have a person in our lives whom we can look up to, we can enjoy that person and try to be like him or her. That is good and healthy.

Can you think of at least one person whose behavior is so good and special that you wish you could be just like him or her one day?

In your diary, list five of your favorite people and the reasons why they are your favorites. Then write about a favorite moment with one of those people. Choose a moment that really describes his or her special ways. When you have done that you have set a goal: to be like your hero. You probably won't become exactly like him or her, but it's the trying that counts.

Heroes are people. No hero is perfect. Remember that when you think about your favorite people. If one of them does something human, forgive him or her. We all make mistakes. Try to remember the wonderful things that make him or her someone to look up to, someone to care about.

ANGER

You may never get completely over your anger at being disabled. That's okay. Anger has a lot of energy behind it. Turn that energy into something useful. If anger keeps welling up even after you have tried hard to get it out (jogging, walking, running, screaming outside, talking with a friend, or writing your emotions down, to name several ways), then try to direct your anger to a useful activity. Ryan White decided to help by educating the public about AIDS. He could have sat at home and watched TV, and some days he probably did. But he decided to use his energies for positive things on the days when he felt better.

Look inside yourself. Are your days filled with frustration? Do you let the frustration build until you have to explode every so often to let it out? How about harnessing that energy by doing something that would make you feel proud of yourself? No examples here, because *you* have to decide. When times are tough and you're angry at the world, work on that special something . . .

FEAR

Perhaps you are the type of person who is never mad, just scared. Are you afraid something *else* will happen to you? If you simply follow your parents' and school's rules, you should be okay. You should be secure.

But no one is really secure. Any one of us could have the roof fall in on us in a heartbeat. Do any of us know what is going to happen to us tomorrow? No. We can follow and understand life's patterns. We can do things and have them come out the same way day in and day out. We see some predictability in the world. But who knows for sure? Not one of us.

If you live with the thought: "If this awful thing happened to me, I had better protect myself from anything else happening," your fear is getting out of control. You simply must admit that next possibility and face it. Often, facing our fears shrinks them. They become smaller because we begin to understand the unknown and find that it's not all that bad. Try it a little at a time at first, and you'll see what facing fear means.

PAUL

I was born with cystic fibrosis. My case has been controlled pretty much by all the great antibiotics we have today. My lungs become infected almost continually by one germ or another. Some days I feel very weak. Other times my antibiotic really helps. During some of my hospital stays when I was little, I learned to play chess with my dad. I remember those games with a warm feeling in my heart, because hospitals are not the warmest places to be. If I found myself feeling strong enough to sit up for even a few minutes, I'd push a pawn around. Everyone at my house knows that if they move just one chessman they are in deep trouble with Dad and me. Sometimes our games last a whole week at home! Anyway, I have started my freshman year in high school, and I hear they have a chess team. I have wanted to be on a chess team ever since I was little, but I've been afraid. When I got really sick I'd have to miss meetings. And after a weak period of my disease, I cough and breathe quite heavily. I don't know. I don't want to gross out the players. Yet I know I could beat the pants off most of those guys. I just have to do it without thinking. If I explain to the chess club adviser, maybe things would be okay. I want to play so bad I can feel the queen in my hand right now!

Are you thinking that Paul should just *do it?* You're right! But he's caught up in his old doubts. He's embarrassed by his handicaps. He doesn't want to put people out. He's scared and afraid.

FREEDOM IS JUST A THOUGHT AWAY

Fear and anger at your life and your disabilities take up a lot of time and energy. They can make you tired. Being tired brings you down. Those feelings can make you miss out on great things. Next time you start thinking the same old fearful or angry thoughts: STOP. Go do your favorite thing and think better thoughts. Think: "See, I'm great at doing this. I love myself when I get time to do this!" Now, if you're in school or somewhere you need to be, don't rush off to do your favorite thing to get your anger under control. Instead, begin to replace your thinking pattern of anger or fear with some inner hugs. Tell yourself, "It's all right to be upset, but I can't leave this situation right now. I know I'm a good person. I know I can do lots of things. After this, I'm going to take time to do my special thing that will make me feel better." For Paul, a game of chess would make him smile, wouldn't it?

If you can replace your angry thoughts with good thoughts and your feelings of fear with good feelings about yourself, you will slowly feel a sense of freedom. You do not *have* to be sad, mad, or afraid. You can choose to set yourself free, free to use your mind in happier ways, free to show the world *you*.

CHAPTER ◇ 1 1

How to Keep a Diary

Writing down your thoughts is an excellent way to learn about them. To some people, writing seems to be something they "don't do." But if you incorporate this healing routine in your life, your mind and soul will be healthier for it. An added bonus is that organizing your thinking into sentences has a magical way of teaching you how to talk to others. All of us can use a little training in how to be better understood.

STEPS TOWARD KEEPING A JOURNAL

Number One

Buy a book with lined or unlined pages. Choose one that appeals to you. It does not have to say "Diary" and have a lock, although locking it may be something you'd like to do. Hardback blank-paged books are available in bookstores everywhere, priced as low as three dollars. You could use a large sketch pad if you like to draw or paint or color. You could date each page, write one or two words, and draw to your heart's content. This journal is to be very personal, an expression of your inner you! Let yourself go when you choose it. Think of it as a treat!

Number Two

Decide to write. If you hate writing, jot down only a few words about your day. As you go along, one day may be one word, the next, several sentences. Think about whom you want to address: Dear Diary, Dear God, Dear Dad, Dear Mom, Dear Me, Dear Cousin, Dear Aunt, Dear Anyone. You do not have to do that, but having a person there in front of you makes the writing like a conversation.

Number Three

Choose a time every day to make your diary entries. The most popular time is five minutes before going to bed, but it does not have to be five minutes. If you've had a particularly active day of growing, you'll find five minutes flies. Stick to it! Bedtime is a great time because almost everyone goes to bed every night, right? If you tell yourself you'll write after school, that's fine. But if a friend drops by, there goes the diary. You have to try very hard to write every day so that it becomes a habit, a habit toward a good healthy mind.

Number Four

Date each entry you make. That is important because one day you'll want to look back on your journey. You'll be surprised to recall when things happened and how you felt about events in your past.

Number Five

Perhaps working with a friend interests you. A close friend or relative might enjoy doing something so personal with you. If you don't mind having another person read your thoughts, the trading of your reading his or hers might make it worth the lack of total privacy. You decide. If the inner you says no, just keep this to yourself, put the journal in a secret place, and tell no one where it is. You could tell your parents that you would prefer for them not to read it right now. They should respect your wishes. However, that does not mean you are giving away all your secrets if you talk about what you wrote in your diary the other day. If you're a private person, that's fine. But talking is not giving it all away.

Well, five steps are all you really need to get started. Below are some sample entries to get you going:

Thursday, July 18, 1989

Dear God,

Well, I started camp. I was nervous. But after the first five minutes I actually met someone really nice that goes to my school. Maybe these next two weeks won't be too awful.

Wed. 6/21/90

Too tired to write
Feel like scribbling
       (scribble, scribble, scribble)

Mon. 9.9.90

I hate my Math teacher. She made me feel dumb today.
       (picture of the awful Math teacher)

5/5/90

Dear (a cousin),

After I'm through writing this in my journal, I'm going to copy it and send it to you. I feel like writing you a letter. That way some of my diary entries will have responses! How did it go at your Junior Prom last month? Was that girl a great date or what? Mine was outstanding . . .

Love,

4/5/90

I am angry.

4/6/90

I don't know why I'm angry.

4/7/90

I'm tired of being mad.

4/8/90

My brother drives me nuts. He always wants to fight.

4/9/90

I've got to figure out a way to stop being mad at my brother.

4/10/90

I tried doing our favorite thing with my brother today. We played ball for about an hour. He told me *twice*, "That's a great catch." I don't feel mad anymore.

4/11/90

I snuck in and made my brother's bed today. You can't *believe* how nice we got along after that! I'm not doing it every day though . . .

A journal is a present you give yourself. It's a way to make your learning curve clearer.

Siblings' Feelings

F ortunately, many physically challenged children have brothers and sisters. It is hard enough to be a disabled person, feeling isolated and sometimes very lonely. Having a brother or sister around can make life more normally focused. What does that mean? Well, sometimes a handicapping situation becomes the main thing a family thinks about. If there are other children in the family, members have to focus their attention at least part of the time on nonhandicap matters. This makes a healthier environment. Living with only one purpose, one problem, can make that problem seem bigger than it really is.

ACCIDENT OR DISEASE VICTIMS

When a trauma occurs, a family is thrown into days, weeks, and months of intense attention to the child hurt. This is necessary to learn about the challenge and care for the child. But it can become very tiresome to the handicapped person's siblings.

WILLIAM

When my sister had to go to the hospital to have a kidney removed, I felt bad for her. But I also thought she was lucky because she could get out of school. My mother taught her all her lessons for about a month. She had whatever she wanted for lunch and watched TV for her school breaks. What a life! I remember going to the hospital to see her right after the operation though. She couldn't even breathe without pain. I guess she deserved the extra fun once she got home. One day I actually faked throwing up just to stay home and share in the fun. My mother was on a leave of absence from her job. We all sat around playing cards and pigging-out. It was the best sick-day I ever had!

William was jealous of the attention given to his sister. That's normal. His mother did him a favor by allowing him to stay home and share in it. Whatever the handicapping event, the other siblings need to feel that they are a part of the family crisis, even if it means staying out of school a day or two. The handicapped person must try very hard to share with brothers or sisters. That brings the family into a healthy understanding of each other's feelings. Jealousy is normal. Being left out hurts.

DAVID

My sister goes to doctors and checkups and therapists all year long. On those days Mom takes her to lunch or takes her shopping. She's always doing special things with her on her appointment days. I hate it. I hate my sister coming home and telling me all about her wonderful afternoon when I have to slave away in the classroom. Sometimes I wish my sister never was born.

David resents the special care his mother takes to have his sister treated well. The resentment is building up and will damage his and his sister's friendship if something isn't done. David should tell his mother how he feels. Then his mother should choose an after-school time and take only David out on an expedition. He is jealous. That is normal. Having Mom to himself will make him feel that he is being treated like his sister, with special kindness and love. It is normal for brothers and sisters to want to feel loved equally. It is difficult for parents of handicapped children because sometimes their time is limited. Feelings sometimes are overlooked. Parents can't read minds.

COMMUNICATION IS A GOLDEN KEY

Communicating feelings to brothers and sisters and parents must become an important daily event in a disabled person's home. Jealousy between sisters, anger between brothers can build up in everyone and result in constant fighting and bickering. Talking things out is never more important than right in your own home.

The person also must be sensitive to the sibling's feelings. It isn't fair if you're the only one who gets a day off from school — no matter what the reason. It isn't fair for the disabled child always to get the first of everything, or the most patience from the parents. Brothers and sisters have feelings. You're not the only person in the world — handicapped or not. Being self-centered to the point of ignoring others' feelings can make your family life a living nightmare.

If your family and your brothers or sisters are all unhappy, perhaps a family counselor should be a part of your lives for a while. If you see a problem, try to talk it out with one of your medical team members; perhaps he would have a suggestion.

SUGGESTIONS FOR GETTING ALONG BETTER

1. Do something for your brother or sister. Make it something you know he or she would love, not something *you* would love. Make her bed, write her a note, do one of her chores for her.
2. Include your sibling in a discussion of your day at the doctor's.
3. Ask, just for the heck of it, about someone whom your brother or sister hangs out with. Be interested in his or her life.
4. Ask your parents if your sibling can go along on your next clinic visit so you can share the day. Point out that an excuse of having personal business is all you need for the teacher. It could turn out to be a wonderful day, and not one person would feel left out!
5. Be a friend to your brother or sister. Look out for his or her feelings. You know your parents; if you see something that hurts your sibling, talk to your parents about it. They probably aren't even aware that they're hurting or bothering him.

Academic Talent

More often than not, physically challenged persons are extremely intelligent. They are gifted in many areas that are sometimes overlooked because of their physical impairment. That is overwhelmingly frustrating for the young person. Nothing is worse than feeling trapped, unrecognized and unappreciated.

Disabled teenagers, even more than adults, are largely ignored. They wait in line for an ice cream, and people just walk ahead of them. Academically stimulating material is often not presented to the handicapped child on the incorrect premise that: "Well, he has enough to do." As a matter of fact, things are frequently done for the handicapped child "just to make life easier."

Nothing is further from the truth. A preschooler can gain nothing when a teacher uses the scissors and cuts things out for him. How will he ever learn if not given the opportunity?

The handicapped person has a right to have a chance at challenging academic materials in school especially. It may take a little longer for him to finish the work physically. That does not mean that his mind cannot handle it.

ASHLEY

I figured out a long time ago — like when I was reading in kindergarten and no one else even knew the letters — that I was highly intelligent. But since I was born with cerebral palsy, I don't look as if I can handle things. My movements are not smooth, and I have difficulty standing on my crutches for long periods. My arms are not always easy to control either. That makes for incredible frustration. But my life is better since I got a computer that I can operate with my voice. My father works for a computer company and got a great discount on this amazing tool. Now that I'm beginning high school, all my reports and homework look fantastic. You'd be amazed how fast I am. I actually feel sorry for the other kids who have to type or handwrite everything! Not me! I've decided to be a writer of some kind. I'm great with words, and I could make enough money to live completely on my own. I'm free! My mind is flying now! My teachers at school are realizing that I can handle any assignment I get. When I'm bored, I just do an extra project and hand it in for extra credit. I'm going to make something out of my life, no matter what!

Ashley certainly has a positive attitude toward her abilities. Sometimes it's difficult to remain positive without having faith in yourself.

The gifted teenager must stick up for herself. She must put her talents out for everyone to see so that she may be assured of a chance to be challenged academically. If school is too easy or too boring, push for testing to see if you belong in a more advanced class. If the tests are timed, and you are physically handicapped, ask your supporting teacher and parents whether the time factor can be extended. Special circumstances require special rules. If you are talented in the arts or music you should be given every extra opportunity. It is the school's job to educate you in the very best way possible.

The Resources list at the back of this book has some addresses that you can write to if you are having trouble getting a proper education. If your school is not bending to meet your needs, every state has laws to support your right to the best education for your specific needs. Handicapped people's organizations around the country are there to help.

Unfortunately, you can feel very much alone through all this, especially if you are sensitive. At times, you can feel like a burden to the teachers and faculty because they have to do something a little extra to help you. Do not dwell on negative people. You are as special and deserving as any other student in your school. If you have to toot your own horn to get attention, go ahead, toot! But be smart about it: toot to the teachers you know are interested in you and your education. These are the specialists who can make your academic career a joy. Look for the teachers who have your welfare in mind. They are the people, because of their commitment to education, who could move a mountain or two for you.

BEGINNING ADULT LIFE

High school is the beginning of your adult life. Try to use the people around you to get the education and challenges you need. If you can be your own strongest supporter, your own hardest worker, you pave your future with golden opportunity.

For many handicapped teenagers, going on to college seems an impossible dream. It is not. But you have to work. You have to study. If you take the college-bound courses and do well, why shouldn't you have a college education of two, three, five, or ten years?

WHAT ARE YOUR CAREER GOALS?

Who would be better qualified to help other disabled people professionally than you, a handicapped person yourself? Take a look around your hospital, institution, clinic, or rehabilitation center. Several handicapped professionals work there. How did they get there? Well, first they received training. Think about the opportunities a person can have if he is educated, specialized, and sensitive toward people's needs.

THE PHYSICALLY CHALLENGED PERSON'S GUIDE TO A FUTURE OF HOPE AND ACCOMPLISHMENT

1. Find a supporter or two or three. Be sensitive to teachers who go out of their way to help you. Become friends with those people. Work hard for them. Show them that your brain is on fire with thoughts!
2. If you are unhappy with your coursework at school, discuss it. It is best to talk with people in the following order (to avoid hurting anyone's feelings and also to alert people who may not know you are discontented):
    a) your parents or guardian;
    b) the teacher of the subject you're concerned about;

    c) your guidance counselor;

    d) your principal.

3. If you do not want to talk to these people alone, ask your parents to go with you. You'll need their help, especially if your school is not interested in mainstreaming. You will need adults if you have to transfer to another school. You may not like that idea, but under the law, public school students must be provided with education to meet whatever special needs exist. Blindness, deafness, academic talent, all types of special needs must be met.

4. If you want to be independent when you get older, some things may have to be done to provide you with the tools to get a well-paying job and establish a life-style of your own. Some school districts consolidate their resources and build one school for an entire region that deals with deafness, for instance. You may have to be bussed out of your area to receive proper education. Don't let any of that stop you from being the best you can possibly be.

5. Begin sending for information. If you want to understand the laws of your state concerning your rights, write to your Congressman or Senator. If you want to know whether colleges provide courses of study you're interested in, write to them. Even if you're still in eighth grade, write for information. Become informed. That way you can plan your life to come out the way you'd like. Ask your strongest supporters: your concerned teachers. They will be able to help you, or at least point you in the right direction. Ask questions, be smart. Use the mind you have!

No matter how frustrating your life may be, there is always a step to be taken toward bettering it. Try some of the guidelines above. Knowledge is the golden key to success. Reading this book is a start.

CHAPTER 14

We, the Leaders

F ollowing the line of thinking in the previous chapter, the well-educated disabled person has a special responsibility. That responsibility is not to be angry at the world for his or her hardships. The very best expert in the field of disabled citizens is *you*! You understand what it means to be disabled. You can take the responsibility of that understanding and educate the rest of your society. If each handicapped person were to use a small part of his energy in educating others, the world of your children would be a more accepting world for challenged people of all kinds. No one else can do this as well as the expert: you!

AN EXCEPTIONAL PRESIDENT

An outstanding example of a leader we all can look up to was President Franklin Roosevelt. Although paralyzed, he led the country through World War II. Read about him in the library sometime; you'll learn that he suffered quite a lot during his later Presidential years. But his intelligence and sense of humor kept our country together.

AN EXCEPTIONAL PATIENT

Dr. Bernie Siegel has a term to define a special kind of patient: "the exceptional patient." That person is one who takes control of his or her life and becomes a leader of his own care. The same principle can be applied to any part of your life, especially if you want to become a leader. You don't have to lead an entire nation as a President does. You could be a leader of a self-help teen group, or a youth group for your church. The point of trying to lead and educate is to help people understand your point of view. That changes people's attitudes toward the disabled. People respected the hard-working Franklin Roosevelt. Do something worthwhile to make people respect you. In that small way you will be lifting prejudice from people's minds.

PREJUDICE

You understand prejudice. You know what it's like to be treated differently because of your outward appearance or behavior. You feel so alone, so left out. Don't be angry about prejudice. Realize that people are not out to make your life difficult; they simply do not understand. Your part in leadership of any group can make a difference. Your role as teacher can change the way people treat you — for the better.

If you want something badly enough, you cannot wait around for somebody else to do it. As you grow older and better educated, the task of overcoming your handicap and becoming a responsible adult will become easier. Things that bothered you three years ago will not seem so awful as you read back those diary entries. You will be you, and you'll have to do something with your life. Make understanding handicapped people a hobby of yours. If you wish there were a self-help group in your community and there isn't one, *start one*! A community church may lend facilities for such a project; or perhaps your hospital or rehab center would lend you a room for meetings. If a group exists, join it and be a leader. Share what you have learned in this book. Show the way to a healthy mind by your strong, healthy example. Some day a young person may think *you're* a hero!

CHAPTER 15

Life Is a Challenge — for Everyone

Know that you are special. You have challenges, handicaps. That is difficult at times; some days your life can overwhelm you. But know this too: Every single person is challenged with his or her own personal problems. Yours may be obvious because it is physical and apparent to others. However, every single human being has something he or she considers a handicap.

Following are a few examples to help you understand the people you consider "normal" or better off than you.

- The overweight person who has little control over her eating.
- The fosterteen who has not had the same home for two years in a row.
- The teenager whose father died when he was nine and he still grieves over his loss.
- The only Vietnamese kid in the whole school.
- The new kid who just moved onto your street.

- The high schooler whose parents divorced, remarried, and divorced again.
- The pregnant teen.

Do you understand? Although you consider yourself special, you should not be so self-centered as to think you are *more* special than your fellow students. You can become your own worst enemy if you choose to think that you've gone through so much more than anybody else that you can go to the front of the line all the time. Fair is fair! Reverse discrimination is not good, ever.

CHAPTER 16

Ways to Face Each Day — with Happiness

There is hope. The future is yours to make as positive as you possibly can. It is yours to begin creating. Medical technology can help. Prosthetists have been perfecting a battery-operated five-fingered electronic prosthesis with a glove that has fingernails you can polish. Computers talk to the sight-impaired. Entire computer-systems are made for quadriplegics that can be run with a stick in the mouth or just the voice. Hundreds of organizations have been formed for the purpose of helping the disabled. Look in your telephone directory. Look at the Resources list at the back of this book. Money is available if equipment or appliances are what you need. You can talk to people who can help you raise enough money to get that corneal transplant, that electric wheel-chair, or that advanced computer software to help you study for your college exams. Your needs can be met. Be your own best friend. Reach out to those who can make a difference in your life by helping you be successful. Show the world you are valuable, and you will be valued. Show your neighborhood that you're willing to work at your life; they will support you. But you must breathe in deep, every day, and fight for your own life. You have been handed a certain number of challenges. Meet them.

Make it your hobby to educate yourself in the newest areas of medicine that affect your particular condition. Read, write, and see professionals who are specialists. Share all this with your family. Your life may be difficult, very difficult. You have the option *every day* to make it better. Make sure of it!

This is the end of this book, but the beginning of a new you. You can reread this book. You can read some of the books in the booklist. Your life is good in many ways. It can always be made better. There are people who understand how you feel. There are many handicapped people. You are not alone. You're you. You may have a disability. *All of us have shortcomings, challenges, handicaps.* But then again, some of the time, we don't.

Glossary

adolescence Period from the beginning of puberty until maturity.

AIDS acquired immune deficiency syndrome caused by the human immunodeficiency virus (HIV); the virus permits infections, malignancies, and neurologic diseases.

amputee Person lacking a limb (finger, hand, arm, foot, leg).

anger Extreme displeasure, desire to lash out, hit. Associated with a loss or death of a loved one or one's own health. May be directed toward family, friends, or medical people responsible for the person's care.

asthma Difficulty breathing because of a spasm of the bronchial tubes and/or mucus in them.

ataxia Defective muscular coordination.

benign Not progressive, not cancerous.

bilateral Affecting both sides.

body-image Picture people have of their physical appearance based on their own view and reactions to others (self-image).

cerebral palsy Paralysis resulting from developmental defects in brain or trauma at birth; movements are often spastic because of lack of control of certain muscles.

challenge To stimulate or excite into action.

chemotherapy Use of chemical medicines to kill disease-causing microorganisms; usually used in cancer treatment.

cleft lip Congenital separation of upper lip; may be associated with cleft palate.

cleft palate Congenital hole in the roof of the mouth, opening the mouth to the nose.

clinic Center for physical exams and treatment of outpatients.

congenital Existing at birth.

counselor   Person usually trained as a health professional who provides advice and guidance for a patient/person's mental and physical well-being.

curve   Line deviating from the straight.

cystic fibrosis   Inherited disease affecting the pancreas and respiratory system; characterized by chronic respiratory infections and other internal problems.

depression   Altered mental mood; loss of interest in pleasurable outlets. Severe cases involve loss of weight, sleeplessness, feelings of worthlessness, lack of energy, overwhelming confusion.

Down's syndrome   Moderate to severe retardation caused by genetic chromosome abnormality; usually an extra 21st or 22nd chromosome.

extremity   Terminal part of something: lower — hip, thigh, leg, ankle, foot; upper — shoulder, arm, forearm, wrist, hand.

grief   Emotional reaction to loss of a loved one or object (or part of body). Physical reactions can include overwhelming fatigue, hollow or empty feeling in chest or abdomen, sighing, shortness of breath, lump in the throat.

handicap   Disadvantage that makes achievement unusually difficult; mental or physical disability.

heterogeneous   Having unlike traits; grouped without regard to differences or similarities; opposite of homogeneous.

homogeneous   Grouped by likeness or sameness of abilities; opposite of heterogeneous.

impairment   Loss or abnormality of physical or mental structure or function.

independent living   Skills to perform daily activities; term used as the end goal of rehabilitation: assuming responsibility for directing one's own life.

legal blindness   Degree of loss of clarity in vision that prevents a person from performing work requiring eyesight; in the U.S., corrected vision of 20/200 or less.

limb   Arm or leg.

mainstreaming   Educational practice of allowing handicapped children to participate in hetereogenous classroom settings.

malignant Cancerous.

multiple sclerosis Inflammatory disease of the nervous system with degradation of the nerves; can go into remission.

myoelectric prosthesis Advanced prosthetic device operated by batteries turned on by electrodes that are attached to muscles; the movement of muscles activates the prosthesis.

oncology Branch of medicine dealing with tumors and cancer.

paranoid Being persistently concerned with one subject, leading to unrealistic thought processes about that subject.

paraplegia Paralysis of lower portion of body and both legs.

prosthesis (pras-THE-sis) Artificial substitute for a missing part such as an artificial extremity or organ.

prosthetics Branch of surgery/medicine dealing with replacement of missing parts.

prosthetist Specialist in making artificial limbs.

psychologist One trained in mental processes and behaviors, analysis, therapy, and research.

psychiatrist Medical doctor trained in the diagnosis, treatment, and prevention of mental illness.

puberty Period in life at which members of both sexes become functionally capable of reproduction.

quadriplegia Paralysis of all four extremities and usually the trunk.

rape Sexual intercourse against the will of the victim.

rehabilitation Process of education and treatment that leads a disabled patient to attain maximum function, a sense of well-being, and a personally satisfying level of independence.

remission Period in which symptons of a disease disappear.

siblings Children of the same parents; brothers and sisters.

spastic Having involuntary sudden movement or convulsive muscular contraction.

spina bifida Congenital defect of walls of spinal canal; lack of union (a hole) between some vertebrae, with spinal cord protruding through the opening, forming a tumor.

transfusion, blood Injection of blood or blood parts such as plasma into the bloodstream.

trauma   Disordered mental or behavioral state resulting from mental or emotional stress or physical injury.

well-being   Sense of wellness, of total mental and physical health.

Resources and Reading List

Ability Magazine
P.O. Box 5311
Mission Hills, CA 91345
  National magazine for amputees.

Adams, B. *Like It Is: Facts and Feelings about Handicaps from Kids You Know.* New York:Walker & Co., 1979.

Allen, George N. *RI.* Englewood Cliffs: Prentice-Hall, 1978. Korean boy with amputation adopted by an American soldier.

Anderson, Peggy. *Children's Hospital.* New York: Harper & Row, 1985.

Area Child Amputee Center
235 Wealthy SE
Grand Rapids, MI 49503
(616) 454 – 7988
  Handbooks for children and adults.

Blank, J. *Nineteen Steps Up the Mountain: The Story of the DeBolt Family.* Philadelphia: J.B. Lippincott, 1976. Story of the founders of Aid to Adoption of Special Kids (AASK).

Brazelton, B.T. *Infants and Mothers* (1969), and *Toddlers and Parents* (1974). New York: Dell Publishing.

Brown, T., and Ortiz, F. *Someone Special Just Like You.* New York: Holt, Rinehart & Wilson, 1984. Photo essay on children with special needs, ages three up.

Buscaglia, Leo. *The Disabled and Their Parents: A Counseling Challenge*. New York: Holt, Rinehart & Wilson, 1983.

————. *Because I Am Human*. Thorofare, NJ: Charles B. Slack, 1972. Photos of children and adults celebrating life.

Butler, D. *Cushla and Her Books*. Boston: Horn Book, 1980. Reading becomes the family's pastime, making Cushla's development the best it could be despite her many physical handicaps.

Deford, Frank. *Alex: The Life of a Child*. Cystic Fibrosis Foundation, P.O. Box 96476, Washington, DC 20077 – 7215.

Desmarowitz, Dorothea. *Martin Is Our Friend*. Nashville, TN: Abingdon Press.
Story of a boy who can't walk but helps children become more sensitive; ages 4 – 10.

Donavan, Peter. *Carol Johnston: The One-Armed Gymnast*. Chicago: Children's Press, Sports Star Series, 1982.
In 1978 Carol placed second in the nation in both balance beam and floor exercises and was named All-American Gymnast.

Dreikurs, R., and Satz, V. *Children: The Challenge*. New York: Hawthorne Books, 1964.

Fanshawe, E. *Rachel*. Scarsdale, NY: Bradbury Press, 1975. Rachel's example of having fun with her wheelchair underlines the sameness of all children as well as the differences; preschool to 8 years.

Fassler, Joan. *Howie Helps Himself*. Riverside, CA: Albert Whitman; NACAC; 3900 Market Street; 1975.
Boy with cerebral palsy who struggles and succeeds.

Featherstone, H. *A Difference in the Family: Life with a Disabled Child*. New York: Basic Books, 1980.
Mother's account of her child's life and others.

Feingold, S.N., and Miller, N. *Your Future: A Guide for the Handicapped Teenager*. New York: Richards Rosen Press, 1982. Realistic and positive approach to living independently.

Fifty-Two Association for the Handicapped, Inc.
441 Lexington Avenue
New York, NY 10017
  Sports association.
Gallaudet College Press
800 Florida Avenue NE
Washington, DC 20002
  Free catalogue for hearing-impaired booklist.

Gliedman, J., and Roth, W. *The Unexpected Minority: Handicapped Children in America*. New York: Harcourt Brace Jovanovich, 1980. Enlightening research for the Carnegie Council on Children.
Goodshell, J. *Daniel Inouye*. New York: Cromwell Publishing, 1977. Distinguished veteran with one arm; U.S. Senator from Hawaii.
Grollman, Sharon. *Shira: A Legacy of Courage*. New York: Doubleday & Company.
Howe, J. *The Hospital Book*. New York: Crown Publishers, 1981.

Institute for the Advancement of Prosthetics
4424 South Pennsylvania Avenue
Lansing, MI 48910 – 5695
(517) 394 – 5850
Publishes newsletter with up-to-date information on prosthetics.

Ilg, F., Ames, L., and Baker, S. *Child Behavior*. New York: Barnes & Noble, 1981.

Imprints
7001 Alonzo Avenue NW
Seattle, WA 98107 – 0625
Newsletter of the Birth & Life Bookstore; excellent source of books on various challenges.

In Stride
Alfred I. duPont Institute
1600 Rockland Road
Wilmington, DE 19899
   Newsletter for parents of children with prostheses; free;
   write for back issues too.

JACPOC
222 South Prospect Avenue
Park Ridge, IL 60068
   *Journal of the Association of Children's Prosthetic-Orthotic
   Clinics*; $15/yr. or $25/2 yrs.

Kamien, Janet. *What If I Couldn't . . . ? A Book about Special
   Needs.* New York: Charles Scribner's Sons, 1979.
   Explanations of specific handicaps: physical immobility, mental
   retardation, blindness, dyslexia, emotional problems.
Kaufman, C. *Rajesh.* New York: Atheneum Books, 1985.
Kegal, B. *Sports for the Leg Amputee*, 1986, Medic Publishing
   Co., P.O. Box 89, Redmont, WA 98073 – 0089.
Litchfield, Ada. *Captain Hook, That's Me.* New York: Walker
   and Company, 1982.
   Elementary-age fictional tale of a little girl with one hand and a
   left hook.
Mack, Nancy. *Tracy.* Milwaukee: Raintree Publisher, 1976.
   About dealing with teasing in a mainstream school.
MacLachlen, P. *Through Grandpa's Eyes.* New York: Harper &
   Row, 1980.
   Grandpa's eyes cannot see, but through their ears, fingers,
   and hearts he and his grandson see in different ways.
McConnell, N. *Different and Alike.* Colorado Springs, CO:
   Current, Inc.
   Discussion of various handicaps; includes a braille alphabet.
McCormick, E. *The Incredible Mr. Kavanaugh.* New York:
   Devin-Adair, 1961.
   True story of a man who accomplished much in spite of the
   absence of arms and legs.

Menotti, Gian-Carlo. *Amahl and the Night Visitors.* New York: McGraw-Hill, 1972.

Set in biblical times, a lame boy shares the Wise Men's journey.

Meyer, D., and Fewell, R. *Living with a Brother or Sister with Special Needs.* Seattle: University of Washington Press, 1985.

Meyers, Jeff. *One of a Kind,* 1980. Sunrise Publishing, 11652 Fairgrove Ind. Boulevard, Maryland Heights, MO 63043.

Story of an amputee football player.

Miezio, P. *Parenting Children with Disabilities: A Professional Source for Physicians and a Guide for Parents,* 1983.

Phoenix Society, Levittown, PA.

National Handicapped Sports and Recreation Association (NHSRA)

Farragut Station, P.O. Box 33141

Washington, DC 20033

Write for chapter nearest you.

Newth, Philip. *Roly Goes Exploring.* New York: Philomel Books, 1981.

Roly the circle is very inquisitive. Shapes are the characters, with braille as well as the printed word.

Nicholson, W. *Pete Gray: One-Armed Major Leaguer.* Englewood Cliffs, NJ: Prentice-Hall, 1976.

Nordic Committee on Disability. *The More We Do Together.* New York: World Rehabilitation Fund, 1985.

PACT (Parents of Amputee Children Together)

Kessler Institute for Rehabilitation

Pleasant Valley Way

West Orange, NJ, 07052

Palestra Magazine

P.O. Box 508

McComb, IL 61455

Programs for the Handicapped

Clearinghouse on the Handicapped

Department of Education/Office of Special Education and
   Rehabilitative Services
Washington, DC 20202
   Periodic newsletter.
Rabe, Berniece. *The Balancing Girl*. New York: E.P. Dutton,
   1981.
   A talented girl shows her teachers and classmates that being in
   a wheelchair is only one thing about her.
Richter, E. *The Teenage Hospital Experience*. New York:
   Cowen, McCann Geoghegan, 1982.
   Specific help and discussion ,of feelings.
Rogers, F. *Josephine the Short-Neck Giraffe*. Pittsburgh: Family
   Communications, Inc., 1975.
   Ages 0 − 10.
Sargent, S., and West, D.A. *My Favorite Place*. Nashville, TN:
   Abingdon Press, 1983.
   Blindness and the other four senses; ages 0–8.
Setoguchi, Y., and Rosenfelder, R. *The Limb-Deficient Child*.
   Springfield, IL: Charles C. Thomas, 1982.
Stein, B. *About Handicaps: An Open Family Book for Parents
   and Children*. New York: Walker and Company, 1984.
Sullivan, Brightman, Blatt, Roberts, and Williams, Fiske.
   Feeling Free. Reading, MA: Addison-Wesley, 1979.
   From the television series. Photos, cartoons, stories, games,
   and puzzles on blindness, cerebral palsy, deafness,
   dwarfism, and learning disabilities.

Superkids Newsletter
60 Clyde Street
Newton, MA 02160
   Highlighting amputee children; free.
Sutcliff, Rose. *Warrior Scarlet*. New York: Henry L. Walch,
   Inc., 1958.
   Young boy with an underdeveloped arm became a great
   warrior 900 years ago; ages 10-up.

Tate, Joan. *Ben and Annie.* New York. Doubleday and Co., 1974.
Friendship with a wheelchair child.

Trull, P. *On with My Life.* New York: Putnam, 1983.
Cancer and amputation.

Voigt, C. *Izzy Willy-Nilly.* New York: Atheneum Books, 1986.
Teenager loses a leg in an accident; identity crisis and adjusting.

Vermont Handicapped Ski Foundation Newsletter
P.O. Box 261
Brownsville, VT 05037

Waller, S. *Circle of Hope.* New York: Evans Publishing Company, 1981.
Family experiences with amputation.

White, Paul. *Janet at School.* New York: Thomas Y. Crowell, 1978.
Wheelchair child with spina bifida; positive story with photos.

Westburg, G. *Good Grief.* Philadelphia: Fortress Press, 1962.
Short book on the grief process.

Whipple, Lee. *Whole Again.* Green Hill Publishers, Box 738, Ottawa, IL 61350.
Story of an adult amputee's search for adequate prosthetic care.

Wolf, B. *Don't Feel Sorry for Paul.* New York: J.B. Lippincott, 1974.
Photos of a boy with multiple prostheses and his accomplishments.

Yolen, Jane. *The Seeing Stick.* New York: Thomas Y. Crowell, 1977.
An emperor gives a fortune to any person who can help his daughter "see."

Index

A

acceptance, of differences, 5
adaptation, 39–45
alone-time, 26, 29
amputee, 1, 11, 12, 13
anger, 7, 10, 11, 13, 17, 22, 23,
    27, 57, 63–67, 74, 82
  energy of, 63–65
arm, broken, 4
asthma, 19–20
ataxia, 20–21
attention
  need for, 15, 78
  negative, 16–17
attitude
  accepting, 17
  changed, 5
  negative, 23–24, 25, 27, 56
  positive, 6, 7, 26, 49, 56, 77

B

behavior, changing, 22–23
blindness, 2, 12, 14, 36–37, 40,
    80
Buscaglia, Leo, 40

C

cancer, 56–57, 61
cerebral palsy, 17–18, 77–78
change
  adolescent, 34–38
  in life, 3, 9, 12, 43–45
  of puberty, 16, 35
chemotherapy, 56–57
church group, 11, 36, 83
cleft palate, 16
club
  chess, 66
  new, 11
college, as possibility, 79, 88
communication, 21–22, 28, 36, 74
computer, 77, 87
cooperation, with medical team,
    60–61
Coping with Death, 50
counselor, 30–31, 35, 40, 47, 75
crutches, 11, 20
crying, 51
cystic fibrosis, 66

D

date rape, 37
dating, 15–16, 34–38
deafness, 15–16, 80
deal, making, 10
death, books on, 52
deformity, facial, 46–48
depression, 7, 12, 25, 30, 48,
    50–52, 56
diary, 6, 23, 31, 64, 68–71, 83
disability, 2, 5, 16, 20, 21, 31, 32,
    35, 39, 42, 76, 87

discrimination, 5
   reverse, 86
doctor, 54, 73
   anger at, 10
   shopping for, 60
   as supporter, 6
   trust in, 58
Down's syndrome, 19
drinking/driving, 50
dyslexia, 34–35

E
education, right to, 78, 80
enemy, doctors as, 54, 56, 57–58
explaining disability, 11, 16, 18,
   27

F
family
   as helpers, 20–21
   as supporters, 6, 35
fear, 55, 63–67
Feel Good Chart, 31
feelings
   of challenged person, 20–21,
      27, 74
   expressing, 22, 23, 35
freedom, 31–32, 67
friends, 16, 17, 28–29, 30–31,
   32–33
   anger at, 10
   making, 18, 27, 29
   sharing diary with, 70
frustration, 11, 65, 77
   adaptation to, 39–45, 81

G
goal
   career, 79
   near-term, 49–50
   setting, 31, 44, 64
   striving toward, 23, 50
grief process, 9–14, 41, 42, 56
guilt, feelings of, 3, 50
gymnastics, 1, 47

H
handicap, 4, 5, 9, 16, 35, 66, 73,
   83, 85
   definition, 2
   learning about, 19, 35, 88
   teaching about, 36
happiness, 10, 24, 29, 46, 51,
   87–88
hearing aid, 15–16
helping challenged person, 17,
   20, 30, 32–33
helplessness, 7, 20, 23
hemophilia, 28–29, 63–65
heroes, 64
hope, 10

I
independence, 30–33, 35, 80
information, obtaining, 6, 80
injury, 3
   automobile, 30, 50
   hunting, 40–41

J
jealousy, 73, 74
joy, 23, 46–47
   inner, 49, 51

K
kindness, 17, 32, 74
   to self-, 2
Kubler-Ross, Elisabeth, 41

L
learning, 5, 24, 40
learning curve, 40–42, 45, 71
life, map of, 42–43
listening, importance of, 48, 51
Living, Loving, and Learning, 40
loner, 28–29
loss, facing, 9, 42
love
    expressing, 21–22, 33
    need for, 15, 35, 74
    self-, 17, 25, 33, 36
Love, Medicine, and Miracles, 63

M
medical personnel, partnership
    with, 53–62
multiple sclerosis, 13–14

N
nerves, degeneration of, 20–21

O
oncology, 56–57

P
paraplegia, 30–31
partnership, healing, 61
patience, 17, 38
patient, 58
    exceptional, 61, 83
Peck, M. Scott, 43
peers, 34–38
prejudice, 83–84
prosthesis, 11, 13, 40, 59, 87
punishment, 10

Q
quadriplegia, 87
questions, asking, 48–49, 59–60

R
Raab, Robert, 50
reality, accepting, 10
responsibility, taking, 23–24, 82
Road Less Traveled, The, 43
Roosevelt, Franklin, 82, 83

S
sadness, 7, 9, 10, 11–12, 21, 22,
    23, 45, 46, 48, 51, 67
school
    new, 11
    problems in, 79–80
scoliosis, 54
self
    expressing, 26–27
    feeling good about, 7
    forgiving, 7
    knowing, 28–51
    liking, 5
    as member of medical team,
        58–60
self-worth, 25–29
shock, 10
siblings, 72–75
Siegel, Bernie, S., 61, 83
sorrow, 10, 46–52
spina bifida, 38
staring, 16, 17–18, 40, 44
suicide, 50
supporters, 6, 79
support group, 35, 84
surgery, 4, 16, 54, 56, 73
    plastic, 46
sympathy, 12, 15–24, 32, 55

T
talent, academic, 76–71

teacher
    challenged person as, 18–20,
        36, 82
    as supporter, 6, 78, 80
team, medical, 58–60, 75
teasing, 11
Thalidomide, 11
therapist, 54, 73
    as supporter, 6
tonsillectomy, 4
transference, 43

trauma, 3–4, 10, 11, 31, 72

U
understanding, 5, 12, 15–24, 36,
        37, 55, 59

W
wheelchair, 11, 13–14, 30, 38, 87
White, Ryan, 63, 65
Why me?, 7, 11, 63